EDGE COMPUTING 101
NOVICE TO PRO

EXPERT TECHNIQUES AND PRACTICAL APPLICATIONS

4 BOOKS IN 1

BOOK 1
EDGE COMPUTING FUNDAMENTALS: A BEGINNER'S GUIDE TO DISTRIBUTED SYSTEMS

BOOK 2
EDGE COMPUTING ARCHITECTURES: DESIGN PRINCIPLES AND BEST PRACTICES

BOOK 3
ADVANCED EDGE COMPUTING: SCALABILITY, SECURITY, AND OPTIMIZATION STRATEGIES

BOOK 4
EDGE COMPUTING IN INDUSTRY 4.0: PRACTICAL APPLICATIONS AND FUTURE TRENDS

ROB BOTWRIGHT

Published by Rob Botwright
Library of Congress Cataloging-in-Publication Data
ISBN 978-1-83938-674-9
Cover design by Rizzo

Disclaimer

The contents of this book are based on extensive research and the best available historical sources. However, the author and publisher make no claims, promises, or guarantees about the accuracy, completeness, or adequacy of the information contained herein. The information in this book is provided on an "as is" basis, and the author and publisher disclaim any and all liability for any errors, omissions, or inaccuracies in the information or for any actions taken in reliance on such information. The opinions and views expressed in this book are those of the author and do not necessarily reflect the official policy or position of any organization or individual mentioned in this book. Any reference to specific people, places, or events is intended only to provide historical context and is not intended to defame or malign any group, individual, or entity. The information in this book is intended for educational and entertainment purposes only. It is not intended to be a substitute for professional advice or judgment. Readers are encouraged to conduct their own research and to seek professional advice where appropriate. Every effort has been made to obtain necessary permissions and acknowledgments for all images and other copyrighted material used in this book. Any errors or omissions in this regard are unintentional, and the author and publisher will correct them in future editions.

BOOK 1 - EDGE COMPUTING FUNDAMENTALS: A BEGINNER'S GUIDE TO DISTRIBUTED SYSTEMS

BOOK 2 - EDGE COMPUTING ARCHITECTURES: DESIGN PRINCIPLES AND BEST PRACTICES

BOOK 3 - ADVANCED EDGE COMPUTING: SCALABILITY, SECURITY, AND OPTIMIZATION STRATEGIES

BOOK 4 - EDGE COMPUTING IN INDUSTRY 4.0: PRACTICAL APPLICATIONS AND FUTURE TRENDS

Introduction

Welcome to "Edge Computing 101: Novice to Pro - Expert Techniques and Practical Applications," a comprehensive book bundle designed to guide you through the intricate world of edge computing from beginner to advanced levels.

In today's digital landscape, where data is generated at an unprecedented rate and real-time processing is crucial, edge computing has emerged as a transformative technology. This book bundle is your gateway to understanding and mastering edge computing, covering everything from its fundamental principles to advanced strategies and real-world applications.

Book 1, "Edge Computing Fundamentals: A Beginner's Guide to Distributed Systems," serves as your starting point, offering a primer on distributed systems and laying the groundwork for understanding the core concepts of edge computing. Whether you're new to the field or seeking to solidify your foundational knowledge, this book provides the essential building blocks to *embark on your journey into the world of edge computing.*

Once you've grasped the fundamentals, Book 2, "Edge Computing Architectures: Design Principles and Best Practices," takes you deeper into the design considerations and architectural patterns essential for building robust and scalable edge computing systems. From deployment models to optimization techniques, this book equips you with the knowledge and tools needed to design effective edge architectures.

Book 3, "Advanced Edge Computing: Scalability, Security, and Optimization Strategies," elevates your understanding by exploring advanced techniques and strategies for overcoming scalability challenges, enhancing security measures, and optimizing performance in edge environments. Through real-world examples and case studies, you'll gain practical insights into tackling complex issues and achieving optimal outcomes in your edge computing deployments.

Finally, Book 4, "Edge Computing in Industry 4.0: Practical Applications and Future Trends," delves into the practical applications of edge computing across various industries, with a focus on Industry

4.0. From manufacturing to healthcare to smart cities, you'll discover how edge computing is revolutionizing processes, driving efficiency, and shaping the future of industry.

Whether you're a novice looking to build a solid foundation or a seasoned professional seeking to stay ahead of the curve, "Edge Computing 101: Novice to Pro" provides you with the knowledge, tools, and insights needed to navigate the complex and dynamic world of edge computing. Join us on this journey as we explore the possibilities, challenges, and opportunities that lie ahead in the realm of edge computing.

BOOK 1
EDGE COMPUTING FUNDAMENTALS
A BEGINNER'S GUIDE TO DISTRIBUTED SYSTEMS

ROB BOTWRIGHT

Chapter 1: Introduction to Edge Computing

Edge computing represents a paradigm shift in the way we process and manage data. It's a distributed computing model that brings computation and data storage closer to the location where it's needed, rather than relying solely on centralized data centers. This proximity to data sources reduces latency and enables real-time processing, making it ideal for applications that require instant responsiveness. At its core, edge computing aims to address the limitations of traditional cloud computing architectures by pushing computation closer to the edge of the network. This concept of "the edge" refers to the outer boundary of the network where data is generated and consumed. By moving computing resources closer to where data is produced, edge computing minimizes the need to transmit data over long distances to centralized servers, thereby reducing latency and bandwidth usage. This approach is particularly advantageous for applications that require low latency and high bandwidth, such as autonomous vehicles, industrial automation, and IoT devices. In essence, edge computing extends the capabilities of the cloud by distributing computing resources across a decentralized network of edge devices. These edge devices can range from smartphones and tablets to IoT sensors and edge servers deployed at the network edge. By leveraging these distributed resources, edge computing enables faster response times, improved reliability, and greater resilience to network failures. From a conceptual standpoint, edge computing can be visualized as a multi-tiered architecture consisting of three main layers: the edge, the fog, and the cloud. At the lowest layer, the edge devices, such as sensors and actuators, collect data from the physical world and perform initial processing tasks. These edge devices are typically constrained in terms of processing power and memory but are capable of capturing data at the source. The next layer, known as the fog or edge gateway, serves as an intermediary between the edge devices and the cloud. It aggregates and filters data from multiple edge devices before forwarding it to the cloud for further analysis. This layer may also host lightweight computing tasks to preprocess data before sending it to the cloud, reducing the amount of data transmitted over the network. Finally, the cloud layer encompasses the centralized data centers where more intensive processing and analysis take place. Here, large-

scale data analytics, machine learning algorithms, and other compute-intensive tasks are executed to derive insights from the aggregated data. Together, these three layers form a hierarchical architecture that balances computational workload and data processing across the network. In practice, deploying edge computing involves a combination of hardware, software, and networking technologies. Edge devices are equipped with sensors, actuators, and computing resources to collect and process data locally. These devices may run lightweight operating systems optimized for edge computing tasks, such as Linux-based distributions tailored for embedded systems. Additionally, edge devices may be configured to communicate with each other and with the cloud using standard networking protocols such as TCP/IP or MQTT. Edge gateways, on the other hand, serve as the bridge between the edge and the cloud, providing connectivity, data aggregation, and preprocessing capabilities. These gateways may be implemented using off-the-shelf hardware or purpose-built appliances equipped with networking interfaces and edge computing software stacks. Depending on the specific use case, edge gateways may support various communication protocols and data formats to integrate with existing infrastructure *and cloud services. When deploying edge computing solutions, organizations must consider factors such as security, scalability, and interoperability. Security measures such as encryption, access control, and secure boot are essential to protect sensitive data and prevent unauthorized access to edge devices and gateways. Scalability is another critical consideration, as edge computing deployments may involve thousands or even millions of edge devices distributed across a wide geographic area. To ensure seamless operation and management of edge infrastructure, organizations may leverage containerization and orchestration technologies such as Docker and Kubernetes. These tools enable the deployment, scaling, and monitoring of edge applications in a standardized and automated manner, simplifying the management of complex edge environments. Interoperability is also key to the success of edge computing initiatives, as heterogeneous devices and systems must be able to communicate and exchange data seamlessly. Standards such as MQTT, CoAP, and OPC UA facilitate interoperability between edge devices, gateways, and cloud services, enabling the development of vendor-agnostic edge solutions. In summary, edge computing represents a fundamental shift in the way we design and* deploy computing infrastructure. By moving computation closer to the edge of the network, edge computing enables faster response times, improved reliability, and greater scalability for a wide range of applications. From smart cities and autonomous vehicles to industrial automation and IoT, edge computing is poised to transform industries and unlock new opportunities for innovation and growth. As organizations continue to embrace edge computing, it's essential to adopt best practices and standards to ensure the security, scalability, and interoperability of edge deployments. Through collaboration and investment in edge computing technologies, we can harness the power of the edge to drive digital transformation and create a more connected and intelligent world.

The historical context of edge computing traces back to the early days of computing. During the mainframe era, computing power was centralized in large, expensive machines located in data centers. As computing technology evolved, so did the need for more distributed architectures. The advent of personal computers and local area networks (LANs) decentralized computing to some extent, allowing organizations to deploy computing resources closer to end-users. However, the rise of the internet and cloud computing brought about a new era of centralized computing, with data and applications hosted in remote data centers operated by cloud service providers. Despite the advantages of cloud computing, such as scalability and cost-effectiveness, it also introduced challenges related to latency, bandwidth constraints, and data privacy. These challenges became more pronounced with the proliferation of IoT devices and the emergence of real-time applications that require instantaneous response times. As a result, there was a growing need for a computing model that could address these challenges by bringing computation closer to the edge of the network. Edge computing emerged as a solution to this problem, offering a decentralized approach to computing that complements traditional cloud computing architectures. The concept of edge computing is not entirely new; it builds upon earlier concepts such as distributed computing, grid computing, and content delivery networks (CDNs). However, what sets edge computing apart is its focus on placing computing resources at the periphery of the network, in close proximity to where data is generated and consumed. This proximity enables edge computing to deliver low-latency, high-bandwidth services that are well-suited for real-time applications such as autonomous vehicles, industrial automation, and augmented reality. The evolution of edge computing can be traced through various milestones in the development of computing technology. One such milestone is the emergence of edge caching and content delivery networks in the late 1990s and early 2000s. Content delivery networks (CDNs) such as Akamai and Cloudflare were among the first to deploy edge servers at strategic locations around the world to cache and deliver content closer to end-users, reducing latency and improving performance. Another milestone in the evolution of edge computing is the rise of edge computing platforms and frameworks. Companies like Amazon Web Services (AWS), Microsoft Azure, and Google Cloud Platform (GCP) have introduced edge computing services that enable developers to deploy and manage edge applications more easily. These platforms provide tools and APIs for deploying, monitoring, and scaling edge applications across distributed infrastructure. The proliferation of IoT devices has also played a significant role in driving the adoption of edge computing. With billions of connected devices generating massive amounts of data, traditional cloud computing architectures struggle to keep up with the volume, velocity, and variety of data generated at the edge. Edge computing provides a solution by enabling data processing and analysis to be performed locally on edge devices or edge servers, reducing the need to transmit data back to centralized data centers for processing. This approach not only reduces latency and bandwidth usage but also improves data privacy and security by keeping sensitive data within the local network. Looking ahead, the future of edge computing is poised to be shaped by advancements in technologies such as 5G, artificial intelligence (AI), and edge-native applications. 5G networks promise to deliver ultra-low latency and high-bandwidth connectivity, enabling new use cases such as remote surgery, autonomous vehicles, and immersive gaming. AI and machine learning algorithms will continue to play a crucial role in edge computing, enabling edge devices to process and analyze data in real-time, extract actionable insights, and make autonomous decisions without relying on centralized servers. Edge-native applications, designed specifically for edge environments, will become more prevalent as developers embrace the unique capabilities and constraints of edge computing. Deploying edge computing solutions involves a combination of hardware, software, and networking technologies. From a hardware perspective, edge devices range from sensors and *actuators to edge servers and gateways. These devices are equipped with computing resources such as CPUs, GPUs, and FPGAs, as well as storage and networking capabilities. On the software side, edge computing applications are typically developed using programming languages such as Python, Java, or C++, and deployed using containerization technologies such as Docker or Kubernetes. These containers encapsulate the application code and its dependencies, making it easier to deploy and manage edge applications across distributed infrastructure. Networking plays a crucial role in edge computing, enabling communication between edge devices, gateways, and cloud services. Networking technologies such as Wi-Fi, Bluetooth, Zigbee, and cellular connectivity are used to connect edge devices to the network, while protocols such as MQTT, CoAP, and HTTP facilitate communication between edge devices and cloud services. In summary, the historical context and evolution of edge computing reflect a gradual shift towards decentralized computing architectures that place computing resources closer to the edge of the network. From its origins in distributed computing and content delivery networks to its current state as a key enabler of real-time applications and IoT, edge computing continues to evolve in response to the changing demands of the digital economy. As organizations increasingly embrace edge computing to drive innovation and unlock new opportunities, it's essential to understand the historical context and evolution of edge computing to fully appreciate its potential impact on the future of computing.*

Chapter 2: Understanding Distributed Systems

Principles of distributed computing form the foundation of modern computing architectures. At its core, distributed computing involves the coordination of multiple computing devices to achieve a common goal. This coordination is essential for handling large-scale data processing tasks, supporting fault tolerance, and enabling scalability. One of the fundamental principles of distributed computing is the concept of decentralization. Decentralization refers to the distribution of computing resources across multiple nodes in a network, rather than relying on a single centralized server. By distributing computing tasks across multiple nodes, decentralized systems can achieve higher reliability and fault tolerance. Another key principle of distributed computing is concurrency. Concurrency allows multiple tasks to execute simultaneously, enabling efficient resource utilization and improving system performance. In distributed systems, concurrency is often achieved through parallelism, where tasks are divided into smaller subtasks and executed in parallel on different nodes. Achieving concurrency requires careful coordination and synchronization of tasks to prevent conflicts and ensure data consistency. Scalability is another important principle of distributed computing. Scalability refers to the ability of a system to handle increasing workloads and resources without sacrificing performance or reliability. Distributed systems are inherently scalable because they can distribute tasks across multiple nodes, allowing them to scale horizontally by adding more nodes to the network. This horizontal scalability enables distributed systems to handle large-scale data processing tasks, such as web servers, databases, and big data analytics platforms. Fault tolerance is another critical principle of distributed computing. Fault tolerance refers to the ability of a system to continue operating in the presence of hardware or software failures. In distributed systems, fault tolerance is achieved through redundancy and replication. By replicating data and computation across multiple nodes, distributed systems can continue operating even if some nodes fail or become unavailable. Achieving fault tolerance requires mechanisms for detecting failures, such as heartbeating or health monitoring, and mechanisms for recovering from failures, such as automatic failover or data replication. Consistency is another important principle of distributed computing. Consistency refers to the property that all nodes in a distributed system see the same data at the same time, regardless of where the data is stored or accessed. Achieving consistency in distributed systems is challenging because of factors such as network latency, node failures, and concurrent updates. Distributed systems typically employ consistency models to define the level of consistency that is acceptable for a given application or use case. These consistency models range from strong consistency, where all nodes see the same data at the same time, to eventual consistency, where updates propagate asynchronously and may take time to converge. Another key principle of distributed computing is isolation. Isolation refers to the property that the execution of one task or transaction does not interfere with the execution of other tasks or transactions. Achieving isolation in distributed systems requires mechanisms for concurrency control and transaction management, such as locks, semaphores, and distributed transactions. These mechanisms ensure that concurrent tasks or transactions can execute safely without interfering with each other. Finally, distributed systems must be designed with security in mind. Security refers to the protection of data, resources, and communications from unauthorized access, disclosure, modification, or destruction. In distributed systems, security is a complex and multifaceted challenge that requires careful consideration of factors such as authentication, authorization, encryption, and access control. Deploying secure distributed systems requires implementing security best practices, such as using strong encryption algorithms, enforcing access controls, and regularly auditing system components for vulnerabilities. In summary, principles of distributed computing are essential for designing, deploying, and managing modern computing architectures. By understanding and applying these principles, developers and system architects can build scalable, fault-tolerant, and secure distributed systems that meet the demands of today's digital economy. Whether deploying web applications, big data analytics platforms, or IoT networks, principles of distributed computing provide a solid foundation for building reliable and resilient systems that can scale to meet the needs of users and businesses alike.

Key components and characteristics of distributed systems are crucial for understanding the architecture and operation of modern computing infrastructures. Distributed systems are composed of multiple interconnected nodes that *communicate and collaborate to achieve a common goal. These nodes can be physical machines, virtual machines, containers, or even software processes running on a network. The primary goal of distributed systems is to harness the collective computational power of multiple nodes to solve complex problems or handle large-scale data processing tasks. One of the key components of distributed systems is communication middleware. Communication middleware provides the necessary infrastructure for nodes to exchange messages, share data, and coordinate their activities. Examples of communication middleware include message queues, publish-subscribe systems, and remote procedure call (RPC) frameworks. These middleware components enable nodes in a distributed system to communicate asynchronously or synchronously, depending on the requirements of the application. Another important component of distributed systems is distributed storage. Distributed storage systems provide a scalable and fault-tolerant mechanism for storing and accessing data across multiple nodes. These systems typically replicate data across multiple nodes to ensure high availability and reliability. Examples of distributed storage systems include distributed file systems, key-value stores, and distributed databases. These systems enable applications to store and retrieve data efficiently, even in the presence of node failures or network partitions. Scalability is a fundamental characteristic of distributed systems. Scalability refers to the ability of a system to handle increasing workloads and resources without sacrificing performance or reliability. Distributed systems achieve scalability by distributing tasks across multiple nodes and adding more nodes to the network as needed. This horizontal scalability enables distributed systems to handle large-scale data processing tasks, such as web servers, databases, and big data analytics platforms. Fault tolerance is another critical characteristic of distributed systems. Fault tolerance refers to the ability of a system to continue operating in the presence of hardware or software failures. Distributed systems achieve fault tolerance by replicating data and computation across multiple nodes, allowing them to tolerate node failures or network partitions. These systems typically employ mechanisms for detecting failures, such as heartbeating or health monitoring, and mechanisms for recovering from failures, such as automatic failover or data replication. Consistency is another important characteristic of distributed systems. Consistency refers to the property that all nodes in a distributed system see the same data at the same time, regardless of where the data is stored or accessed. Achieving consistency in distributed systems is challenging because of factors such as network latency, node failures, and concurrent updates. Distributed systems typically employ consistency models to define the level of consistency that is acceptable for a given application or use case. These consistency models range from strong consistency, where all nodes see the same data at the same time, to eventual consistency, where updates propagate asynchronously and may take time to converge. Isolation is another key characteristic of distributed systems. Isolation refers to the property that the execution of one task or transaction does not interfere with the execution of other tasks or transactions. Achieving isolation in distributed systems requires mechanisms for concurrency control and transaction management, such as locks, semaphores, and distributed transactions. These mechanisms ensure that concurrent tasks or transactions can execute safely without interfering with each other. Security is also a critical characteristic of distributed systems. Security refers to the protection of data, resources, and communications from unauthorized access, disclosure, modification, or destruction. In distributed systems, security is a complex and multifaceted challenge that requires careful consideration of factors such as authentication, authorization, encryption, and access control. Deploying secure distributed systems requires implementing security best practices, such as using strong encryption algorithms, enforcing access controls, and regularly auditing system components for vulnerabilities. In summary, key components and characteristics of distributed systems are essential for understanding the architecture and operation of modern computing infrastructures. By understanding and applying these components and characteristics, developers and system architects can design, deploy, and manage scalable, fault-tolerant, and secure distributed systems that meet the demands of today's digital economy. Whether deploying web applications, big data analytics platforms, or IoT networks, key components and characteristics of distributed systems provide a solid foundation for building reliable and resilient systems that can scale to meet the needs of users and businesses alike.*

Chapter 3: Evolution of Computing Architectures

The shift from centralized to decentralized computing represents a significant milestone in the history of computing. In the early days of computing, computing power was centralized in large, expensive mainframe computers located in data centers. These mainframes served as the backbone of computing infrastructure, handling all data processing tasks for organizations and businesses. However, this centralized model had its limitations, including high costs, limited scalability, and single points of failure. As computing technology advanced, new paradigms emerged that challenged the dominance of centralized computing. One such paradigm was distributed computing, which sought to distribute computing tasks across multiple nodes in a network. Distributed computing offered several advantages over centralized computing, including improved scalability, fault tolerance, and performance. By distributing computing tasks across multiple nodes, distributed systems could handle larger workloads and provide greater resilience to hardware failures. The emergence of local area networks (LANs) and personal computers (PCs) further accelerated the adoption of distributed computing. LANs enabled multiple computers to communicate and share resources within a local network, while PCs provided individuals and small businesses with affordable computing power. These developments paved the way for a more decentralized approach to computing, where computing resources were distributed across multiple nodes in a network. Another important milestone in the shift from centralized to decentralized computing was the emergence of the internet. The internet revolutionized the way people communicate, collaborate, and access information, enabling the creation of decentralized applications and services. With the rise of the internet, computing power became increasingly distributed, with data and applications hosted on servers distributed around the world. This distributed model enabled new forms of collaboration and innovation, such as social media, e-commerce, and cloud computing. Cloud computing represents the culmination of the shift from centralized to decentralized computing. In a cloud computing model, computing resources are provisioned on-demand and delivered over the internet, allowing organizations to scale their infrastructure dynamically and pay only for what they use. Cloud computing offers several advantages over traditional centralized computing models, including greater flexibility, scalability, and cost-effectiveness. Organizations can deploy applications and services in the cloud without having to invest in expensive hardware or infrastructure, making it easier to innovate and respond to changing market conditions. However, despite the benefits of cloud computing, there are still challenges associated with centralization, including concerns about data privacy, security, and vendor lock-in. These challenges have led to a renewed interest in decentralized computing paradigms, such as edge computing and blockchain. Edge computing brings computing resources closer to the edge of the network, enabling real-time processing and analysis of data generated by IoT devices, sensors, and other edge devices. By distributing computing tasks across edge devices, organizations can reduce latency, improve reliability, and enhance privacy and security. Blockchain, on the other hand, is a decentralized ledger technology that enables secure, transparent, and tamper-proof record-keeping. By decentralizing data storage and processing, blockchain eliminates the need for centralized authorities and intermediaries, enabling peer-to-peer transactions and collaboration. Together, edge computing and blockchain represent the next frontier in computing, offering new opportunities for decentralization and innovation. As organizations continue to adopt these technologies, they will need to carefully consider the trade-offs between centralization and decentralization, weighing factors such as performance, scalability, security, and privacy. In summary, the shift from centralized to decentralized computing has been a transformative journey, driven by advances in technology and changing business needs. From the early days of mainframe computing to the rise of cloud computing and beyond, the evolution of computing reflects a broader trend towards decentralization and distributed architectures. As we look to the future, it's clear that decentralized computing will play an increasingly important role in shaping the way we work, communicate, and interact with technology. Whether through edge computing, blockchain, or other emerging technologies, decentralization offers new opportunities for innovation and collaboration, paving the way for a more decentralized and interconnected world.

The emergence of edge computing represents a significant evolution in modern architectural paradigms. As technology advances and the demand for real-time processing increases, traditional centralized computing architectures face challenges in meeting the requirements of latency-sensitive applications. Edge computing addresses these challenges by bringing computation closer to the edge of the network, where data is generated and consumed. This proximity enables faster response times, reduces latency, and improves the overall performance of applications. At its core, edge computing extends the capabilities of traditional cloud computing architectures by distributing computing resources across a decentralized network of edge devices. These devices can range from smartphones and IoT sensors to edge servers deployed at the network edge. By leveraging these distributed resources, edge computing enables organizations to process and analyze data closer to the source, minimizing the need to transmit data over long distances to centralized data centers. This approach is particularly advantageous for applications that require low latency, such as autonomous vehicles, industrial automation, and augmented reality. The emergence of edge computing is driven by several factors, including the proliferation of IoT devices, the growth of real-time applications, and the limitations of traditional cloud computing architectures. IoT devices generate vast amounts of data that need to be processed and analyzed in real-time, making traditional cloud computing architectures ill-suited for many IoT applications. Edge computing offers a solution by enabling data processing and analysis to be performed locally on edge devices or edge servers, reducing the need to transmit data back to centralized data centers for processing. This approach not only reduces latency and bandwidth usage but also improves data privacy and security by keeping sensitive data within the local network. The growth of real-time applications, such as video streaming, online gaming, and financial trading, has further fueled the adoption of edge computing. These applications require low latency and high bandwidth to deliver a seamless user experience, making edge computing an attractive solution for deploying compute resources closer to end-users. Additionally, the limitations of traditional cloud computing architectures, such as network congestion, bandwidth constraints, and data sovereignty issues, have led organizations to explore alternative approaches to computing. Edge computing offers a decentralized alternative to traditional cloud computing architectures, enabling organizations to overcome these limitations and deliver faster, more responsive services to their users. From a architectural perspective, edge computing can be visualized as a multi-tiered architecture consisting of three main layers: the edge, the fog, and the cloud. At the edge layer, edge devices such as sensors, smartphones, and IoT devices collect data from the physical world and perform initial processing tasks. These edge devices are typically constrained in terms of processing power and memory but are capable of capturing data at the source. The fog layer, also known as the edge gateway, serves as an intermediary between the edge and the cloud. It aggregates and filters data from multiple edge devices before forwarding it to the cloud for further analysis. This layer may also host lightweight computing tasks to preprocess data before sending it to the cloud, reducing the amount of data transmitted over the network. Finally, the cloud layer encompasses the centralized data centers where more intensive processing and analysis take place. Here, large-scale data analytics, machine learning algorithms, and other compute-intensive tasks are executed to derive insights from the aggregated data. Together, these three layers form a hierarchical architecture that balances computational workload and data processing across the network. Deploying edge computing solutions involves a *combination of hardware, software, and networking technologies. Edge devices are equipped with sensors, actuators, and computing resources to collect and process data locally. These devices may run lightweight operating systems optimized for edge computing tasks, such as Linux-based distributions tailored for embedded systems. Additionally, edge devices may be configured to communicate with each other and with the cloud using standard networking protocols such as TCP/IP or MQTT. Edge gateways, on the other hand, serve as the bridge between the edge and the cloud, providing connectivity, data aggregation, and preprocessing capabilities. These gateways may be implemented using off-the-shelf hardware or purpose-built appliances equipped with networking interfaces and edge computing software stacks. Depending on the specific use case, edge gateways may support various communication protocols and data formats to integrate with existing infrastructure and cloud services. Overall, the emergence of edge computing represents a paradigm shift in modern architectural paradigms, enabling organizations to deploy compute resources closer to the edge of the network and deliver faster, more responsive services to their users. As organizations continue to embrace edge computing, it's essential to understand the architectural principles and deployment considerations involved in designing and deploying edge computing solutions. Through collaboration and investment in edge computing technologies, organizations can unlock new opportunities for innovation and deliver transformative experiences to their users.*

Chapter 4: Basics of Edge Computing Infrastructure

Edge computing infrastructure comprises several components that work together to enable real-time processing and analysis of data at the network edge. At the heart of edge computing infrastructure are edge devices, which include sensors, actuators, and other IoT devices that collect data from the physical world. These edge devices are equipped with computing resources, such as CPUs, GPUs, and FPGAs, to perform local data processing and analysis. Edge devices may also have storage capabilities to store data temporarily before transmitting it to the cloud or edge server. Edge servers are another key component of edge computing infrastructure. These servers are deployed at the network edge to provide additional computing power and storage capacity for processing and analyzing data. Edge servers may be deployed in various locations, such as factory floors, retail stores, or remote sites, depending on the specific use case and requirements. Edge servers are typically equipped with more powerful hardware than edge devices, including multicore processors, high-speed networking interfaces, and solid-state drives (SSDs) for storage. Additionally, edge servers may run specialized software stacks optimized for edge computing tasks, such as containerization platforms like Docker or Kubernetes. Edge gateways play a crucial role in edge computing infrastructure by providing connectivity, data aggregation, and preprocessing capabilities. These gateways serve as the bridge between the edge devices and the cloud or edge server, aggregating and filtering data from multiple edge devices before forwarding it to the cloud for further analysis. Edge gateways may also host lightweight computing tasks to preprocess data before sending it to the cloud, reducing the amount of data transmitted over the network. From a networking perspective, edge computing infrastructure relies on standard networking protocols such as TCP/IP, MQTT, or CoAP to enable communication between edge devices, gateways, and cloud services. These protocols facilitate the transmission of data over wired or wireless networks, ensuring seamless connectivity and interoperability across distributed infrastructure. In addition to networking protocols, edge computing infrastructure may leverage security mechanisms such as encryption, access control, and secure boot to protect data and devices from unauthorized access or tampering. These security mechanisms are essential for ensuring the integrity, confidentiality, and availability of data in edge computing environments. Deploying edge computing infrastructure involves a combination of hardware, software, and networking technologies. From a hardware perspective, organizations must select edge devices, servers, and gateways that meet the specific requirements of their use case. This may involve evaluating factors such as processing power, memory, storage capacity, and connectivity options. Once the hardware components are selected, organizations must install and configure the necessary software stacks to enable edge computing functionality. This may include operating systems, middleware, application frameworks, and security software. Organizations may also need to develop or deploy edge applications that run on edge devices or servers to perform specific tasks, such as data collection, processing, or analysis. Finally, organizations must configure and manage the networking infrastructure to ensure seamless communication between edge devices, gateways, and cloud services. This may involve configuring network interfaces, routing tables, firewalls, and other networking components to optimize performance, reliability, and security. Overall, edge computing infrastructure comprises a complex ecosystem of hardware, software, and networking technologies that work together to enable real-time processing and analysis of data at the network edge. By leveraging edge computing infrastructure, organizations can unlock new opportunities for innovation, efficiency, and competitiveness in today's digital economy. Edge node architecture and deployment models are fundamental to understanding how edge computing operates within distributed systems. At its core, edge computing extends the capabilities of traditional cloud computing by bringing computational resources closer to the data source, enabling real-time processing and analysis. The architecture of an edge node typically consists of three main components: hardware, software, and networking infrastructure. From a hardware perspective, edge nodes are equipped with computing resources such as CPUs, GPUs, and memory to perform local data processing and analysis. These resources may vary depending on the specific use case and requirements of the application. Additionally, edge nodes may have storage capabilities, such as solid-state drives (SSDs) or hard disk drives (HDDs), to store data locally before transmitting it to the cloud or edge server. From a software perspective, edge nodes run specialized software stacks optimized for edge computing tasks. This software may include operating systems, middleware, application frameworks, and edge computing platforms. These software stacks enable edge nodes to perform tasks such as data collection, preprocessing, analysis, and decision-making autonomously, without relying on centralized servers. Networking infrastructure plays a crucial role in edge node architecture, enabling communication between edge nodes, gateways, and cloud services. Edge nodes may be connected to the network via wired or wireless interfaces, such as Ethernet, Wi-Fi, or cellular connectivity. Additionally, edge nodes may use standard networking protocols such as TCP/IP, MQTT, or CoAP to transmit data over the network. The deployment models of edge nodes vary depending on factors such as the specific use case, requirements, and constraints of the application. One common deployment model is the standalone edge node, where edge nodes operate independently and perform all tasks locally without relying on external resources. This deployment model is well-suited for applications that require low latency, high availability, and autonomy, such as industrial automation, autonomous vehicles, and augmented reality. Another deployment model is the edge node with cloud backup, where edge nodes perform local processing and analysis but also transmit data to the cloud for backup, archiving, or further analysis. This deployment model provides a balance between local processing and centralized storage, enabling organizations to leverage the scalability and flexibility of the cloud while maintaining low latency and high reliability at the edge. Yet another deployment model is the edge node with edge server, where edge nodes offload intensive processing tasks to nearby edge servers for additional computing power and storage capacity. This deployment model is well-suited for applications that require high computational intensity or large-scale data processing, such as video analytics, machine learning, and big data analytics. The deployment of edge nodes involves several steps, including selecting hardware, configuring software, and deploying networking infrastructure. Organizations must carefully evaluate factors such as processing power, memory, storage capacity, and connectivity options when selecting edge node hardware. Once the hardware is selected, organizations must install and configure the necessary software stacks to enable edge computing functionality. This may involve installing operating systems, middleware, application frameworks, and edge computing platforms on the edge node. Additionally, organizations must configure the networking infrastructure to ensure seamless communication between edge nodes, gateways, and cloud services. This may involve configuring network interfaces, routing tables, firewalls, and other networking components to optimize performance, reliability, and security. In summary, edge node architecture and deployment models play a crucial role in enabling edge computing within distributed systems. By understanding the components and deployment models of edge nodes, organizations can design and deploy edge computing solutions that meet the specific requirements of their use cases and unlock new opportunities for innovation, efficiency, and competitiveness in today's digital economy.

Chapter 5: Edge Computing Use Cases and Applications

Industry-specific applications of edge computing are revolutionizing various sectors by enhancing efficiency, reliability, and scalability. In manufacturing, edge computing enables real-time monitoring and optimization of production processes, leading to increased productivity and reduced downtime. By deploying edge nodes on factory floors, manufacturers can collect data from sensors and machines, analyze it locally, and make timely decisions to improve operational efficiency. For example, edge computing can enable predictive maintenance by detecting anomalies in equipment performance and triggering maintenance actions before failures occur. In retail, edge computing is transforming the customer experience by enabling personalized recommendations, inventory management, and in-store analytics. Retailers can deploy edge nodes in stores to analyze customer behavior, track inventory levels, and optimize store layouts in real-time. By processing data locally, retailers can provide faster response times and reduce reliance on centralized servers, leading to improved customer satisfaction and loyalty. In transportation and logistics, edge computing is revolutionizing fleet management, route optimization, and supply chain visibility. By deploying edge nodes on vehicles, trucks, and shipping containers, transportation companies can track assets in real-time, optimize delivery routes, and monitor environmental conditions such as temperature and humidity. This enables organizations to improve the efficiency of their logistics operations, reduce fuel consumption, and minimize delays. In healthcare, edge computing is transforming patient care, remote monitoring, and medical imaging. Healthcare providers can deploy edge nodes in hospitals, clinics, and patient homes to collect and analyze vital signs, medical images, and patient data in real-time. By processing data locally, healthcare organizations can improve the accuracy and timeliness of diagnoses, reduce patient wait times, and enhance the quality of care. In agriculture, edge computing is revolutionizing precision farming, crop monitoring, and livestock management. Farmers can deploy edge nodes in fields and barns to collect data from sensors, drones, and satellites, analyze it locally, and make data-driven decisions to optimize crop yields and animal health. By processing data locally, farmers can reduce reliance on internet connectivity and cloud services, enabling them to operate in remote or rural areas with limited connectivity. In energy and utilities, edge computing is transforming grid management, renewable energy integration, and predictive maintenance. Utilities can deploy edge nodes on power plants, substations, and renewable energy installations to collect data from sensors and meters, analyze it locally, and optimize energy production and distribution. By processing data locally, utilities can improve grid stability, reduce energy losses, and minimize downtime, leading to cost savings and environmental benefits. In summary, industry-specific applications of edge computing are revolutionizing various sectors by enabling real-time data processing, analysis, and decision-making at the network edge. By deploying edge nodes in manufacturing, retail, transportation, healthcare, agriculture, energy, and utilities, organizations can unlock new opportunities for innovation, efficiency, and competitiveness in today's digital economy. Whether improving production processes, enhancing customer experiences, or optimizing resource management, edge computing is reshaping industries and driving the next wave of digital transformation. Novel use cases and emerging applications in *various sectors are driving innovation and transforming industries in unprecedented ways. In healthcare, telemedicine is emerging as a novel use case for delivering remote medical care and consultations using telecommunications technology. Patients can connect with healthcare providers via video calls, chat platforms, or mobile apps to receive diagnoses, prescriptions, and treatment recommendations without the need for in-person visits. Telemedicine enables healthcare organizations to reach underserved populations, improve patient access to care, and reduce healthcare costs. Another emerging application in healthcare is wearable technology, which includes devices such as fitness trackers, smartwatches, and medical sensors that monitor health metrics such as heart rate, blood pressure, and blood glucose levels. These wearable devices enable individuals to track their health and wellness in real-time, empowering them to make informed decisions about their lifestyle and healthcare. Wearable technology also enables healthcare providers to remotely monitor patients' health, detect early signs of illness or deterioration, and intervene proactively to prevent complications. In agriculture, precision farming is revolutionizing crop management, soil conservation, and resource optimization. By leveraging sensors, drones, and satellite imagery, farmers can collect data on soil moisture, nutrient levels, and crop health to make data-driven decisions about irrigation, fertilization, and pest control. Precision farming enables farmers to maximize crop yields, minimize input costs, and reduce environmental impact, leading to sustainable and profitable farming practices. Another emerging application in agriculture is vertical farming, which involves growing crops in vertically stacked layers using controlled environment agriculture techniques such as hydroponics, aeroponics, and aquaponics. Vertical farming enables farmers to produce high-quality, fresh produce year-round, regardless of climate or geographical location. By growing crops indoors in vertical structures, farmers can optimize land use, conserve water, and reduce the carbon footprint of food production. In manufacturing, additive manufacturing, also known as 3D printing, is emerging as a disruptive technology for producing complex parts and components with unprecedented precision and efficiency. 3D printing enables manufacturers to create custom-designed products on-demand, reduce lead times, and eliminate the need for expensive tooling and molds. By layering materials such as plastics, metals, and ceramics, additive manufacturing enables manufacturers to produce parts with intricate geometries and superior mechanical properties, opening up new possibilities for product design and innovation. Another emerging application in manufacturing is digital twinning, which involves creating virtual replicas of physical assets, processes, and systems using sensor data, simulation models, and machine learning algorithms. Digital twinning enables manufacturers to monitor and optimize the performance of equipment, predict maintenance needs, and simulate "what-if" scenarios to improve operational efficiency and productivity. By combining real-time data from sensors with advanced analytics and visualization tools, manufacturers can gain insights into their operations, identify opportunities for improvement, and optimize their processes in real-time. In transportation, autonomous vehicles are revolutionizing the way people and goods are transported, enabling safer, more efficient, and more convenient mobility solutions. By leveraging sensors, cameras, and artificial intelligence algorithms, autonomous vehicles can navigate roads, detect obstacles, and make driving decisions without human intervention. Autonomous vehicles have the potential to reduce traffic congestion, improve road safety, and increase access to transportation for people with* disabilities or limited mobility. Another emerging application in transportation is urban air mobility, which involves using electric vertical takeoff and landing (eVTOL) aircraft to provide on-demand aerial transportation services in urban areas. Urban air mobility enables people to bypass traffic congestion and travel quickly and efficiently between destinations, reducing travel times and improving productivity. By integrating eVTOL aircraft with existing transportation infrastructure and digital platforms, urban air mobility providers can offer seamless, multimodal transportation solutions that meet the diverse needs of urban travelers. In energy, renewable energy sources such as solar, wind, and hydroelectric power are emerging as sustainable alternatives to fossil fuels for generating electricity. By harnessing natural resources such as sunlight, wind, and water, renewable energy technologies can produce clean, renewable electricity with minimal environmental impact. Renewable energy sources enable utilities to reduce greenhouse gas emissions, mitigate climate change, and diversify their energy portfolios, leading to a more sustainable and resilient energy future. Another emerging application in energy is energy storage, which involves storing excess energy generated from renewable sources for later use. Energy storage *technologies such as batteries, pumped hydro, and compressed air enable utilities to store surplus energy during periods of low demand and discharge it during peak demand periods, reducing the need for fossil fuel-based power plants and improving grid reliability. By integrating energy storage with renewable energy sources, utilities can optimize their energy resources, balance supply and demand, and improve grid stability, leading to a more efficient and resilient energy system. In summary, novel use cases and emerging applications in various sectors are driving innovation and transforming industries in unprecedented ways. From healthcare and agriculture to manufacturing, transportation, and energy, these applications enable organizations to leverage technology to solve complex challenges, improve efficiency, and create new opportunities for growth and prosperity. By embracing innovation and investing in emerging technologies, organizations can stay ahead of the curve and position themselves for success in the rapidly evolving digital economy.*

Chapter 6: Challenges in Edge Computing

Latency and bandwidth constraints are critical considerations in the design and deployment of distributed systems, impacting performance, scalability, and user experience. Latency refers to the delay between the initiation of a request and the response received, often measured in milliseconds. In distributed systems, latency can be influenced by various factors, including network distance, processing time, and queuing delays. High latency can result in sluggish response times, leading to poor user experience and reduced productivity. Bandwidth, on the other hand, refers to the maximum rate at which data can be transmitted over a network, typically measured in bits per second. Bandwidth constraints can limit the amount of data that can be transferred between nodes in a distributed system, impacting throughput and scalability. In distributed systems, achieving low latency and high bandwidth is essential for delivering real-time services, such as video streaming, online gaming, and financial trading. To mitigate latency and bandwidth constraints, organizations can employ various strategies, including edge computing, content delivery networks (CDNs), and data compression techniques. Edge computing brings computational resources closer to the edge of the network, enabling real-time processing and analysis of data at the source. By deploying edge nodes in proximity to end-users or devices, organizations can reduce the distance data needs to travel, minimizing latency and improving response times. Additionally, edge computing enables organizations to offload processing tasks from centralized servers to edge nodes, reducing bandwidth usage and improving network efficiency. Content delivery networks (CDNs) are another effective strategy for mitigating latency and bandwidth constraints in distributed systems. CDNs consist of a network of servers distributed geographically, caching content and delivering it to users from the nearest edge location. By caching content closer to end-users, CDNs reduce the distance data needs to travel, improving response times and reducing latency. CDNs also offload bandwidth usage from origin servers, enabling organizations to serve content to a large number of users simultaneously without overloading the network. Data compression techniques can also help mitigate latency and bandwidth constraints in distributed systems. By compressing data before transmission,

organizations can reduce the amount of data sent over the network, improving throughput and reducing latency. Compression algorithms such as gzip, deflate, and brotli can be used to compress text-based data such as HTML, CSS, and JavaScript files, reducing file sizes and improving load times for web pages and applications. Additionally, media compression techniques such as H.264, H.265, and VP9 can be used to compress audio and video files, reducing bandwidth usage and improving streaming performance. Deploying these techniques often involves configuring web servers or CDN providers to enable compression for specific types of content. In summary, latency and bandwidth constraints are critical considerations in the design and deployment of distributed systems. By employing strategies such as edge computing, content delivery networks, and data compression techniques, organizations can mitigate these constraints, improve performance, and deliver seamless user experiences. Whether delivering real-time services, serving content to a global audience, or optimizing network efficiency, addressing latency and bandwidth constraints is essential for building scalable, resilient, and high-performance distributed systems.
Data management and synchronization in edge

environments pose unique challenges due to the distributed nature of edge computing architectures. In traditional centralized systems, data management is relatively straightforward, with data stored and processed in a single location. However, in edge environments, data is generated and processed at the network edge, often across a geographically dispersed infrastructure. This decentralized approach to data management introduces complexities related to data consistency, availability, and synchronization. One of the primary challenges in edge environments is ensuring data consistency across distributed nodes. With data being generated and processed at multiple edge locations simultaneously, maintaining consistency becomes challenging, especially in the presence of network latency and communication failures. Inconsistent data can lead to errors, data loss, and incorrect decision-making, undermining the reliability and integrity of edge computing applications. To address this challenge, organizations can implement data synchronization mechanisms that ensure data consistency across distributed nodes. These mechanisms may include distributed databases, consensus algorithms, and conflict resolution strategies that reconcile conflicting updates and maintain a consistent view of the data. For example, distributed databases such as Apache Cassandra or CockroachDB can replicate data across multiple nodes and ensure consistency through techniques such as quorum-based replication and eventual consistency. Consensus algorithms such as Raft or Paxos can be used to coordinate updates and ensure consistency in distributed systems by reaching agreement among nodes on the order of operations. Conflict resolution strategies such as last-write-wins or timestamp-based ordering can be employed to resolve conflicts between concurrent updates and ensure data consistency across distributed nodes. Another challenge in edge environments is managing data availability and access control across distributed nodes. With data being generated and processed at the network edge, ensuring timely access to data becomes critical for supporting real-time decision-making and analysis. However, ensuring data availability can be challenging, especially in environments with intermittent connectivity or limited bandwidth. Additionally, enforcing access control policies to restrict access to sensitive data adds another layer of complexity to data management in edge environments. To address these challenges, organizations can implement data replication and caching strategies that ensure data availability and reduce latency in edge environments. By replicating data across multiple edge nodes and caching frequently accessed data locally, organizations can minimize the impact of network latency and ensure timely access to data for edge computing applications. Additionally, organizations can leverage access control mechanisms such as role-based access control (RBAC) or attribute-based access control (ABAC) to enforce fine-grained access control policies and protect sensitive data in edge environments. These access control mechanisms can be implemented using identity and access management (IAM) solutions such as Keycloak or Auth0, which provide centralized control over user authentication and authorization in distributed environments. Furthermore, organizations can implement encryption and data masking techniques to protect data at rest and in transit, ensuring data confidentiality and integrity in edge environments. By encrypting sensitive data and masking personally identifiable information (PII), organizations can minimize the risk of data breaches and unauthorized access in edge computing applications. Deploying encryption and data masking techniques often involves configuring encryption algorithms and key management policies to encrypt data before *storing it in distributed databases or transmitting it over the network. In summary, data management and synchronization in edge environments present unique challenges due to the distributed nature of edge computing architectures. Addressing these challenges requires implementing data synchronization mechanisms, managing data availability and access control, and deploying encryption and data masking techniques to ensure data integrity, confidentiality, and availability in edge computing applications. By adopting these strategies, organizations can overcome the complexities of data management in edge environments and unlock the full potential of edge computing for real-time decision-making, analysis, and innovation.*

Chapter 7: Security Considerations in Distributed Systems

The threat landscape in distributed systems is complex and constantly evolving, posing significant challenges to organizations deploying and managing distributed infrastructure. Distributed systems, by their nature, are comprised of multiple interconnected nodes, making them vulnerable to a wide range of security threats and attacks. One of the primary threats facing distributed systems is malware, malicious software designed to infiltrate, disrupt, or damage computer systems and networks.

Malware can take various forms, including viruses, worms, trojans, ransomware, and spyware, each with its own methods of propagation and attack. To protect against malware threats, organizations must deploy antivirus software, intrusion detection systems, and network firewalls to detect and mitigate malicious activity in distributed systems. Another significant threat in distributed systems is unauthorized access, where attackers gain unauthorized access to sensitive data, systems, or networks. Unauthorized access can occur through various means, including weak passwords, misconfigured access controls, and software vulnerabilities. To mitigate the risk of unauthorized access, organizations must implement strong authentication mechanisms, such as multi-factor authentication (MFA) and biometric authentication, to verify the identity of users and devices accessing distributed systems. Additionally, organizations must regularly audit and update access control policies to ensure that only authorized users have access to sensitive data and resources. Distributed denial-of-service (DDoS) attacks pose another significant threat to distributed systems, where attackers flood a network or server with a high volume of traffic, causing it to become overwhelmed and unavailable to legitimate users. DDoS attacks can disrupt business operations, degrade network performance, and result in financial losses for organizations.

To mitigate the risk of DDoS attacks, organizations can deploy DDoS mitigation services, such as cloud-based scrubbing centers, that filter and block malicious traffic before it reaches the network. Additionally, organizations can implement rate limiting and traffic shaping techniques to prioritize legitimate traffic and mitigate the impact of DDoS attacks on distributed systems. Data breaches are a pervasive threat in distributed systems, where attackers gain unauthorized access to sensitive data, such as customer information, intellectual property, and financial records. Data breaches can have severe consequences for organizations, including regulatory fines, reputational damage, and loss of customer trust. To protect against data breaches, organizations must implement data encryption, data masking, and data loss prevention (DLP) techniques to secure sensitive data at rest and in transit.

Additionally, organizations must regularly audit and monitor access to sensitive data, detect anomalous behavior, and respond promptly to security incidents to minimize the impact of data breaches on distributed systems. Insider threats pose another significant security risk to distributed systems, where authorized users intentionally or unintentionally misuse their privileges to compromise the security of the system. Insider threats can take various forms, including data theft, sabotage, and fraud, each with its own motivations and methods of attack. To mitigate the risk of insider threats, organizations must implement access controls, monitoring tools, and employee training programs to detect and prevent unauthorized activities by insiders. Additionally, organizations must enforce least privilege principles, where users are granted only the minimum level of access necessary to perform their job functions, to minimize the risk of insider threats in distributed systems. In summary, the threat landscape in distributed systems is diverse and dynamic, posing significant challenges to organizations deploying and managing distributed infrastructure.

By understanding the various threats and implementing appropriate security measures, organizations can mitigate the risks and protect their distributed systems from security breaches, data loss, and other security incidents. Securing edge computing environments requires a comprehensive approach that addresses the unique challenges and vulnerabilities associated with distributed systems. One of the best practices for securing edge computing environments is to establish a strong perimeter defense strategy. This involves deploying firewalls, intrusion detection systems, and access control mechanisms to monitor and control traffic entering and exiting the edge network. CLI commands such as iptables or firewalld can be used to configure firewall rules *and filter incoming and outgoing traffic based on predefined criteria. Additionally, organizations should implement network segmentation to isolate critical assets and sensitive data from the rest of the network, reducing the attack surface and limiting the impact of potential breaches. Another best practice for securing edge computing environments is to encrypt data both at rest and in transit. This involves implementing encryption algorithms such as AES or RSA to secure sensitive data stored on edge devices and transmitted over the network.*

CLI commands such as openssl can be used to generate cryptographic keys, encrypt data, and configure secure communication channels between edge nodes. Additionally, organizations should implement secure protocols such as HTTPS or SSL/TLS to encrypt data transmitted between edge devices and cloud services, ensuring confidentiality and integrity. Patch management is another critical best practice for securing edge computing environments. Organizations should regularly update and patch edge devices, operating systems, and software applications to address known vulnerabilities and mitigate the risk of exploitation by attackers. CLI commands such as apt or yum can be used to install security updates and patches on Linux-based edge devices, while tools such as Windows Update can be used to update Windows-based edge devices. Additionally, organizations should implement vulnerability scanning and penetration testing to identify and remediate security weaknesses in edge computing environments proactively. Access control is another essential best practice for securing edge computing environments. Organizations should implement strong authentication mechanisms such as multi-factor authentication (MFA) and biometric authentication to verify the identity of users and devices accessing edge resources. CLI commands such as ssh-keygen can be used to generate SSH key pairs for secure authentication between edge devices and remote servers.

Additionally, organizations should enforce least privilege principles, where users are granted only the minimum level of access necessary to perform their job functions, to minimize the risk of unauthorized access and privilege escalation. Regular monitoring and auditing are essential best practices for securing edge computing environments. Organizations should deploy monitoring tools such as intrusion detection systems (IDS) and security information and event management (SIEM) systems to monitor network traffic, detect suspicious activities, and generate alerts in real-time. CLI commands such as tcpdump or Wireshark can be used to capture and analyze network traffic on edge devices, while SIEM solutions such as Splunk or ELK Stack can be used to aggregate and correlate security events from multiple sources. Additionally, organizations should conduct regular security audits and assessments to evaluate the effectiveness of security controls, identify gaps and weaknesses, and make informed decisions about improving security posture. Employee training and awareness are critical best practices for securing edge computing environments.

Organizations should provide comprehensive security awareness training to employees, contractors, and partners to educate them about security risks, threats, and best practices. CLI commands such as sudo can be used to restrict access to sensitive commands and resources, while user training programs can educate users about the importance of password hygiene, phishing awareness, and social engineering prevention. Additionally, organizations should establish clear security policies and procedures governing the use of edge devices, data handling practices, and incident response protocols to ensure compliance and accountability. In summary, securing edge computing environments requires a multi-layered approach that addresses the unique challenges and vulnerabilities associated with distributed systems. By implementing best practices such as perimeter defense, encryption, patch management, access control, monitoring, auditing, employee training, and awareness, organizations can mitigate security risks and protect their edge computing environments from cyber threats and attacks.

Chapter 8: Scalability and Performance Optimization Techniques

Scaling strategies for edge infrastructures are essential for ensuring the reliability, performance, and scalability of distributed systems deployed at the network edge. One of the key strategies for scaling edge infrastructures is to design for horizontal scalability, where additional resources can be added dynamically to accommodate increasing workload demands. CLI commands such as Docker Swarm or Kubernetes can be used to deploy containerized applications across multiple edge nodes, automatically scaling resources up or down based on demand. Additionally, organizations can implement auto-scaling policies that monitor resource utilization metrics such as CPU, memory, and network bandwidth and scale resources dynamically to meet performance targets. Another scaling strategy for edge infrastructures is to leverage distributed caching and content delivery networks (CDNs) to reduce latency and improve performance. By caching frequently accessed data and content at the network edge, organizations can minimize the need to retrieve data from centralized servers, reducing latency and improving responsiveness for edge computing applications. CLI commands such as Redis or Memcached can be used to deploy distributed caching solutions that store data in memory and serve it to edge nodes on-demand. Additionally, organizations can leverage CDNs to distribute content such as static web pages, images, and videos to edge servers located closer to end-users, reducing latency and improving load times for web applications. Edge computing also enables organizations to leverage edge storage solutions to store and process data locally at the network edge, reducing reliance on centralized storage infrastructure and improving data locality. By deploying edge storage solutions such as distributed file systems or object storage platforms, organizations can store data closer to where it is generated and consumed, reducing latency and improving data access times for edge computing applications. CLI commands such as MinIO or Ceph can be used to deploy distributed storage solutions that replicate data across multiple edge nodes, ensuring high availability and durability. Additionally, organizations can implement data tiering policies that automatically migrate data between edge nodes and centralized storage based on access patterns and storage requirements. Edge infrastructures can also benefit from the use of edge computing platforms and frameworks that abstract the complexity of distributed systems and provide tools and services for deploying, managing, and scaling edge applications. Platforms such as AWS IoT Greengrass or Microsoft Azure IoT Edge enable organizations to develop and deploy edge applications using familiar programming languages and development tools, while abstracting the underlying infrastructure and scaling challenges. CLI commands such as AWS CLI or Azure CLI can be used to interact with edge computing platforms and deploy edge applications to distributed nodes. Additionally, organizations can leverage edge orchestration frameworks such as Kubernetes Edge or OpenStack Edge Computing to manage and orchestrate containerized applications across distributed edge nodes, ensuring consistency and scalability across the edge infrastructure. Another scaling strategy for edge infrastructures is to implement edge analytics and machine learning algorithms that process and analyze data locally at the network edge, reducing the need to transmit large volumes of data to centralized servers for analysis. By deploying edge analytics solutions such as Apache Kafka or TensorFlow Lite, organizations can perform real-time analytics and inferencing on streaming data from edge devices, enabling faster insights and decision-making. CLI commands such as Apache Kafka CLI or TensorFlow Lite Converter can be used to deploy and manage edge analytics solutions on distributed nodes. Additionally, organizations can implement federated learning techniques that train machine learning models collaboratively across distributed edge devices, aggregating model updates locally and preserving data privacy and security. In summary, scaling strategies for edge infrastructures are essential for ensuring the reliability, performance, and scalability of distributed systems deployed at the network edge. By designing for horizontal scalability, leveraging distributed caching and CDNs, deploying edge storage solutions, using edge computing platforms and frameworks, implementing edge analytics and machine learning algorithms, organizations can scale their edge infrastructures to meet the growing demands of edge computing applications and unlock new opportunities for innovation and efficiency.

Performance tuning and optimization in edge computing systems are crucial for maximizing the efficiency, responsiveness, and scalability of distributed applications deployed at the network edge. One of the key strategies for optimizing performance in edge computing systems is to minimize latency, the delay between the initiation of a request and the receipt of a response, by reducing network round-trip times and processing overhead. CLI commands such as traceroute or ping can be used to measure network latency and identify potential bottlenecks in the communication path between edge devices and backend servers. Additionally, organizations can deploy edge computing nodes closer to end-users and devices to reduce the physical distance data needs to travel, minimizing latency and improving responsiveness for edge applications. Another performance tuning strategy for edge computing systems is to optimize resource utilization and allocation, ensuring that edge nodes have sufficient compute, memory, and storage resources to handle workload demands efficiently. CLI commands such as top or htop can be used to monitor resource utilization metrics such as CPU usage, memory usage, and disk I/O on edge nodes, identifying resource-intensive processes and potential performance bottlenecks. Additionally, organizations can implement resource allocation policies that dynamically allocate resources to edge applications based on demand, ensuring optimal performance and scalability. Edge caching is another effective strategy for performance tuning and optimization in edge computing systems, where frequently accessed data and content are cached locally at edge nodes to reduce latency and improve responsiveness. By caching data closer to where it is consumed, organizations can minimize the need to retrieve data from centralized servers, reducing network overhead and improving application performance. CLI commands such as Varnish or Squid can be used to deploy caching proxies that cache content at edge nodes and serve it to end-users on-demand. Additionally, organizations can leverage content delivery networks (CDNs) to distribute content such as static web pages, images, and videos to edge servers located closer to end-users, further reducing latency and improving load times for web applications. Another performance tuning strategy for edge computing systems is to optimize data transmission and communication protocols to minimize overhead and maximize throughput. By using efficient data serialization formats such as Protocol Buffers or MessagePack, organizations can reduce the size of data transmitted over the network, minimizing bandwidth usage and improving transmission speed. CLI commands such as curl or wget can be used to measure network throughput and identify potential bottlenecks in the communication path between edge devices and backend servers. Additionally, organizations can implement compression techniques such as gzip or brotli to compress data before transmission, further reducing bandwidth usage and improving network performance. Load balancing is another critical strategy for performance tuning and optimization in edge computing systems, where incoming requests are distributed evenly across multiple edge nodes to prevent overloading and maximize resource utilization. By deploying load balancers such as HAProxy or nginx, organizations can distribute incoming traffic to edge nodes based on predefined algorithms such as round-robin, least connections, or IP hash, ensuring optimal performance and scalability. CLI commands such as systemctl or service can be used to start, stop, or restart load balancer services on edge nodes. Additionally, organizations can implement dynamic load balancing techniques that adjust the distribution of traffic in real-time based on changing workload conditions, ensuring that resources are allocated efficiently and performance is optimized. In summary, performance tuning and optimization are essential for maximizing the efficiency, responsiveness, and scalability of edge computing systems. By *minimizing latency, optimizing resource utilization, leveraging edge caching, optimizing data transmission protocols, implementing load balancing, organizations can improve the performance of their edge applications and deliver seamless user experiences to end-users.*

Chapter 9: Edge Computing Technologies and Frameworks

Edge computing platforms play a pivotal role in facilitating the development, deployment, and management of distributed applications at the network edge. These platforms provide developers and organizations with the tools, services, and infrastructure needed to build and operate edge computing solutions efficiently. One of the key components of edge computing platforms is edge orchestration, which enables organizations to manage and orchestrate edge nodes and applications across distributed locations. CLI commands such as Docker Swarm or Kubernetes can be used to deploy and manage containerized applications on edge nodes, ensuring consistency and scalability across the edge infrastructure. Additionally, edge orchestration frameworks such as OpenStack Edge Computing or AWS IoT Greengrass provide tools and services for managing edge deployments, automating tasks such as provisioning, scaling, and monitoring. Edge computing platforms also offer edge analytics capabilities, allowing organizations to perform real-time analysis and inferencing on data generated at the network edge. By deploying edge analytics solutions such as Apache Kafka or TensorFlow Lite, organizations can gain insights and make decisions based on streaming data from edge devices, enabling faster responses and improved efficiency. CLI commands such as Apache Kafka CLI or TensorFlow Lite Converter can be used to deploy and manage edge analytics solutions on distributed nodes. Furthermore, edge computing platforms provide edge storage solutions that enable organizations to store and process data locally at the network edge. By deploying distributed storage solutions such as MinIO or Ceph, organizations can store data closer to where it is generated and consumed, reducing latency and improving data access times for edge applications. CLI commands such as MinIO CLI or Ceph CLI can be used to configure and manage edge storage solutions on distributed nodes. In addition to edge orchestration, analytics, and storage, edge computing platforms offer a range of services and tools for developing and deploying edge applications. These include edge SDKs (Software Development Kits), which provide developers with libraries, APIs, and tools for building and testing edge applications, as well as edge runtime environments, which enable developers to deploy and run applications on edge devices. CLI commands such as AWS CLI or Azure CLI can be used to interact with edge computing platforms and deploy edge applications to distributed nodes. Furthermore, edge computing platforms often provide integration with cloud services, enabling organizations to seamlessly extend their existing cloud infrastructure to the network edge. By leveraging cloud-edge integration, organizations can leverage the scalability, flexibility, and reliability of the cloud while harnessing the low latency and data locality benefits of edge computing. CLI commands such as Terraform or Ansible can be used to automate the deployment and configuration of cloud-edge integration solutions, ensuring consistency and reliability across distributed environments. In summary, edge computing platforms play a critical role in enabling organizations to build, deploy, and manage distributed applications at the network edge. By providing tools, services, and infrastructure for edge orchestration, analytics, storage, application development, and cloud-edge integration, these platforms empower organizations to unlock the full potential of edge computing and drive innovation at the network edge.

In the landscape of edge computing, various

frameworks and tools have emerged to address the unique challenges and requirements of distributed computing at the network edge. One of the prominent frameworks in this space is Apache Kafka, an open-source distributed event streaming platform designed for building real-time data pipelines and streaming applications. CLI commands such as Kafka Connect or Kafka Streams can be used to deploy and manage Kafka clusters, ingest data from edge devices, and process data streams in real-time. Kafka's distributed architecture and fault-tolerant design make it well-suited for edge computing applications that require high throughput, low latency, and seamless scalability. Another popular framework for edge computing is TensorFlow Lite, a lightweight machine learning framework designed for deploying machine learning models on edge devices with limited computational resources. TensorFlow Lite enables organizations to perform inferencing on edge devices, allowing for real-time analysis and decision-making without the need for round-trip communication to centralized servers. CLI commands such as TensorFlow Lite Converter can be used to convert TensorFlow models into optimized formats for deployment on edge devices, ensuring efficient resource utilization and minimal latency.

Additionally, TensorFlow Lite provides support for hardware acceleration through libraries such as TensorFlow Lite for Microcontrollers, enabling organizations to leverage specialized hardware accelerators for accelerated inferencing on edge devices. OpenFaaS (Functions as a Service) is another framework that has gained traction in the edge computing space, providing a serverless computing platform for deploying and running functions at the network edge. CLI commands such as faas-cli can be used to deploy functions to edge nodes, scale resources dynamically based on demand, and monitor function performance in real-time. OpenFaaS's lightweight and modular architecture makes it well-suited for edge computing applications that require fast startup times, low resource overhead, and rapid scalability. Additionally, OpenFaaS provides support for event-driven architectures, enabling organizations to trigger functions in response to events generated by edge devices or external systems. Another framework worth mentioning in the context of edge computing is Apache NiFi, a powerful data flow management system designed for collecting, processing, and distributing data across distributed systems. CLI commands such as nifi-cli can be used to deploy and manage NiFi clusters, create data pipelines for ingesting and *processing data from edge devices, and monitor data flow in real-time. NiFi's graphical user interface (GUI) and drag-and-drop interface make it easy for developers and operators to design and deploy data pipelines without writing code, speeding up development and deployment cycles for edge computing applications. Additionally, NiFi provides support for data provenance, encryption, and access control, ensuring data integrity, confidentiality, and compliance in edge computing environments. In the realm of edge computing tools, one notable solution is AWS IoT Greengrass, a managed edge computing service that extends AWS's cloud capabilities to edge devices. CLI commands such as AWS CLI can be used to deploy Greengrass core devices, configure device groups and subscriptions, and manage edge deployments from the command line. Greengrass enables organizations to run AWS Lambda functions, Docker containers, and machine learning models on edge devices, enabling local processing, data caching, and real-time decision-making at the network edge. Additionally, Greengrass provides seamless integration with other AWS services such as AWS IoT Core, Amazon S3, and AWS Lambda, enabling organizations to build end-to-end edge computing solutions that span from edge devices to the cloud. Another prominent edge computing* tool is Azure IoT Edge, a fully managed service from Microsoft Azure that enables organizations to deploy and manage containerized workloads on edge devices. CLI commands such as Azure CLI can be used to deploy IoT Edge devices, deploy modules to edge devices, and monitor device health and performance from the command line. Azure IoT Edge provides support for deploying Azure services such as Azure Functions, Azure Stream Analytics, and Azure Machine Learning on edge devices, enabling organizations to perform real-time analytics, machine learning inferencing, and event processing at the network edge. Additionally, Azure IoT Edge provides built-in security features such as device authentication, data encryption, and access control, ensuring the integrity, confidentiality, and availability of data in edge computing environments. In summary, the landscape of edge computing frameworks and tools is diverse and rapidly evolving, with each offering unique capabilities and advantages for building, deploying, and managing edge computing applications. From Apache Kafka and TensorFlow Lite to OpenFaaS and Apache NiFi, organizations have a wide range of options to choose from when it comes to selecting the right framework or tool for their edge computing needs. By understanding the strengths and weaknesses of *each framework and tool, organizations can make informed decisions and build scalable, reliable, and efficient edge computing solutions that meet their business requirements and drive innovation at the network edge.*

Chapter 10: Future Trends in Edge Computing

Predicting the evolution of edge computing requires careful consideration of current trends, technological advancements, and emerging use cases in the field. One prediction for the evolution of edge computing is the continued proliferation of edge devices and sensors across various industries and sectors. CLI commands such as Ansible or Terraform can be used to automate the deployment and provisioning of edge devices, ensuring consistency and scalability across distributed environments. As the Internet of Things (IoT) continues to grow, more organizations will deploy edge devices to collect, process, and analyze data at the network edge, enabling real-time insights and decision-making. Additionally, edge computing platforms and frameworks will evolve to meet the growing demand for edge computing solutions, providing developers with more tools, services, and infrastructure for building and deploying edge applications. Another prediction for the evolution of edge computing is the integration of edge computing with other emerging technologies such as 5G, artificial intelligence (AI), and blockchain. CLI commands such as Kubernetes or Docker can be used to deploy containerized applications that leverage AI and machine learning algorithms for inferencing and decision-making at the network edge. With the rollout of 5G networks, organizations will have access to higher bandwidth and lower latency connections, enabling new use cases such as real-time video analytics, augmented reality, and autonomous vehicles. Additionally, blockchain technology can be used to secure and authenticate data transactions between edge devices, ensuring data integrity and trust in edge computing environments. Edge computing will also play a crucial role in enabling edge-to-cloud integration, where edge devices and cloud services work together seamlessly to deliver end-to-end solutions. CLI commands such as AWS CLI or Azure CLI can be used to interact with edge computing platforms and cloud services, enabling organizations to build hybrid edge-cloud architectures that leverage the scalability and flexibility of the cloud while harnessing the low latency and data locality benefits of edge computing. By integrating edge devices with cloud services, organizations can offload compute-intensive tasks to the cloud while performing real-time processing and analysis at the network edge, ensuring optimal performance and scalability for *edge applications. Furthermore, edge computing will drive the adoption of new deployment models and architectures, such as fog computing and multi-access edge computing (MEC), which extend the capabilities of edge computing to the network edge and beyond. CLI commands such as Apache OpenWhisk or OpenStack can be used to deploy serverless functions and edge computing nodes at the network edge, enabling organizations to distribute compute, storage, and networking resources across distributed locations. Fog computing extends the principles of edge computing to the network edge, enabling organizations to deploy edge devices and services in close proximity to end-users and devices, reducing latency and improving performance for edge applications. MEC, on the other hand, extends the capabilities of edge computing to the radio access network (RAN) of mobile networks, enabling organizations to deploy edge services and applications at base stations and cell towers, closer to mobile users and devices. In summary, the evolution of edge computing will be driven by advancements in technology, the proliferation of edge devices and sensors, the integration with other emerging technologies, and the adoption of new deployment models and architectures. By staying abreast of these trends and developments,* organizations can capitalize on the opportunities presented by edge computing and drive innovation at the network edge. Emerging technologies are playing a pivotal role in shaping the future of edge computing, ushering in a new era of innovation and transformation at the network edge. One of the most significant emerging technologies driving the evolution of edge computing is 5G, the fifth generation of cellular networks, which promises to deliver unprecedented speed, bandwidth, and connectivity to edge devices and applications. CLI commands such as Ansible or Terraform can be used to automate the deployment and provisioning of edge devices, ensuring seamless integration with 5G networks and maximizing the benefits of low latency and high throughput. With 5G, organizations can deploy edge applications that require real-time communication and ultra-low latency, such as autonomous vehicles, augmented reality, and industrial automation, unlocking new opportunities for innovation and efficiency. Another emerging technology shaping the future of edge computing is artificial intelligence (AI) and machine learning (ML), which enable edge devices to process and analyze data locally, without the need for round-trip communication to centralized servers. CLI commands such as TensorFlow Lite Converter can be used to convert machine learning models into optimized formats for deployment on edge devices, ensuring efficient resource utilization and minimal latency. By deploying AI and ML models on edge devices, organizations can perform real-time analytics, inferencing, and decision-making at the network edge, enabling new use cases such as predictive maintenance, anomaly detection, and personalized recommendations. Additionally, AI-powered edge devices can adapt and learn from their environment, improving performance and efficiency over time, and enabling autonomous operation in dynamic and unpredictable environments. Edge computing is also being shaped by the Internet of Things (IoT), a network of interconnected devices and sensors that collect, process, and transmit data to centralized servers or edge computing nodes. CLI commands such as Docker or Kubernetes can be used to deploy containerized applications that integrate with IoT devices and sensors, enabling organizations to build scalable and flexible edge computing solutions. With the proliferation of IoT devices, organizations can collect vast amounts of data from various sources, such as smart sensors, wearables, and industrial equipment, enabling real-time monitoring, analysis, and control of physical assets and processes. Additionally, edge computing enables organizations to perform data preprocessing and filtering at the network edge, reducing the volume of data transmitted to centralized servers and minimizing bandwidth usage and latency. Blockchain technology is another emerging technology that is shaping the future of edge computing, enabling secure and transparent transactions between edge devices and external systems. CLI commands such as Hyperledger Fabric or Ethereum CLI can be used to deploy blockchain networks and smart contracts on edge devices, ensuring data integrity, authenticity, and trust in edge computing environments. By leveraging blockchain technology, organizations can establish a decentralized and tamper-proof ledger of transactions, enabling secure and auditable communication between edge devices and external entities. Additionally, blockchain can be used to implement decentralized identity and access management systems, enabling secure and privacy-preserving authentication and authorization of edge devices and users. Edge computing is also being shaped by advances in edge hardware and architecture, such as edge processors, accelerators, and memory technologies, which enable edge devices to perform complex computations and process large volumes of data locally. CLI commands such as *lspci* or *lscpu* can be used to view hardware specifications and identify compatible hardware components for edge computing deployments. With the advancement of edge hardware, organizations can deploy edge applications that require high performance and low power consumption, such as real-time video analytics, autonomous drones, and industrial robotics, unlocking new possibilities for edge computing in diverse industries and sectors. In summary, emerging technologies such as 5G, AI and ML, IoT, blockchain, and edge hardware are shaping the future of edge computing, enabling organizations to build scalable, efficient, and secure edge computing solutions that drive innovation and transformation at the network edge. By leveraging these technologies, organizations can unlock new opportunities for real-time insights, intelligent automation, and immersive experiences, delivering value to customers and stakeholders in a rapidly evolving digital landscape.

BOOK 2
EDGE COMPUTING ARCHITECTURES
DESIGN PRINCIPLES AND BEST PRACTICES

ROB BOTWRIGHT

Chapter 1: Understanding Edge Computing Architectures

Architectural components form the foundation of edge computing systems, encompassing hardware, software, and network elements that work together to enable distributed computing at the network edge. CLI commands such as Docker or Kubernetes can be used to deploy containerized applications that run on edge nodes, ensuring consistency and scalability across distributed environments. At the core of edge computing systems are edge devices, which include sensors, actuators, gateways, and embedded systems that collect, process, and transmit data to centralized servers or edge computing nodes. CLI commands such as lspci or lscpu can be used to view hardware specifications and identify compatible hardware components for edge computing deployments. Edge devices are typically equipped with processing capabilities, storage capacity, and network connectivity, enabling them to perform computation and analysis locally and communicate with other devices and systems in the network. Edge nodes, also known as edge servers or edge gateways, act as intermediaries between edge devices and centralized servers, aggregating, processing, and forwarding data between the two. CLI commands such as SSH or SCP can be used to remotely access edge nodes and deploy applications or updates, ensuring seamless integration with edge computing systems. Edge nodes are often deployed in close proximity to edge devices, reducing latency and improving performance for edge computing applications. Additionally, edge nodes provide services such as data caching, preprocessing, and filtering, enabling organizations to optimize bandwidth usage and reduce the volume of data transmitted to centralized servers. Edge computing systems also include centralized servers or cloud infrastructure, which provide storage, computation, and networking services to edge nodes and devices. CLI commands such as AWS CLI or Azure CLI can be used to interact with edge computing platforms and cloud services, enabling organizations to build hybrid edge-cloud architectures that leverage the scalability and flexibility of the cloud while harnessing the low latency and data locality benefits of edge computing. Centralized servers are typically deployed in data centers or cloud regions, where they can scale resources dynamically to meet changing workload demands and provide high *availability and reliability for edge computing applications. Additionally, centralized servers host edge computing platforms and frameworks that enable organizations to develop, deploy, and manage edge applications efficiently. Networking infrastructure is another critical component of edge computing systems, providing connectivity between edge devices, edge nodes, and centralized servers. CLI commands such as traceroute or ping can be used to measure network latency and identify potential bottlenecks in the communication path between edge devices and backend servers. Networking infrastructure includes wired and wireless technologies such as Ethernet, Wi-Fi, cellular, and LPWAN (Low-Power Wide-Area Network), which enable communication between devices and systems in the network. Additionally, networking infrastructure includes routers, switches, and gateways that route data packets between different network segments and enforce security policies to protect against unauthorized access and malicious attacks. Security is a paramount concern in edge computing systems, given the distributed nature of the infrastructure and the diverse range of devices and systems involved. CLI commands such as nmap or netstat can be used to scan for open ports and identify potential security vulnerabilities in edge devices and nodes. Security measures include encryption, authentication, access control, and intrusion detection, which help organizations protect sensitive data and prevent unauthorized access to edge computing systems. Additionally, organizations can implement security best practices such as regular software updates, patch management, and network segmentation to mitigate security risks and ensure the integrity, confidentiality, and availability of data in edge computing environments. In summary, architectural components form the backbone of edge computing systems, providing the foundation for distributed computing at the network edge. By leveraging edge devices, edge nodes, centralized servers, networking infrastructure, and security measures, organizations can build scalable, efficient, and secure edge computing solutions that drive innovation and transformation in diverse industries and sectors. Taxonomy of edge computing architectures is essential for understanding the diverse approaches and configurations used in deploying distributed computing systems at the network edge. CLI commands such as Docker or Kubernetes can be used to deploy containerized applications that run on edge nodes, ensuring consistency and scalability across distributed environments. Edge computing architectures can be classified based on various factors, including topology, hierarchy, resource allocation, and data processing models. One common taxonomy of edge computing architectures is based on the physical location and proximity of edge devices and nodes to end-users and data sources. CLI commands such as ping or traceroute can be used to measure network latency and identify potential bottlenecks in the communication path between edge devices and backend servers. In a hierarchical edge computing architecture, edge devices are organized into multiple tiers or layers based on their proximity to end-users and data sources. Edge nodes at the network edge process and analyze data locally, reducing latency and improving performance for edge applications. CLI commands such as SSH or SCP can be used to remotely access edge nodes and deploy applications or updates, ensuring seamless integration with edge computing systems. In contrast, centralized servers or cloud infrastructure provide storage, computation, and networking services to edge nodes and devices. CLI commands such as AWS CLI or Azure CLI can be used to interact with edge computing platforms and cloud services, enabling organizations to build hybrid edge-cloud architectures that leverage the scalability and flexibility of the cloud while* harnessing the low latency and data locality benefits of edge computing. Another taxonomy of edge computing architectures is based on the data processing model and distribution of computing resources across edge nodes. Edge computing architectures can be classified into centralized, decentralized, and distributed architectures based on how computing resources are allocated and managed across edge nodes. In a centralized edge computing architecture, computing resources are concentrated in a central location, such as a data center or cloud region, where edge nodes communicate with centralized servers to perform computation and analysis. CLI commands such as top or htop can be used to monitor resource utilization metrics such as CPU usage, memory usage, and disk I/O on edge nodes, identifying resource-intensive processes and potential performance bottlenecks. Decentralized edge computing architectures distribute computing resources across multiple edge nodes, allowing for greater scalability and fault tolerance. Edge nodes operate autonomously and communicate with each other to perform distributed computation and analysis, enabling organizations to build resilient and scalable edge computing solutions. CLI commands such as Ansible or Terraform can be used to automate the deployment and provisioning of edge devices, ensuring consistency and scalability across distributed environments. Distributed edge computing architectures take decentralization a step further, distributing computing resources and decision-making capabilities across a network of edge nodes and devices. CLI commands such as Apache OpenWhisk or OpenStack can be used to deploy serverless functions and edge computing nodes at the network edge, enabling organizations to distribute compute, storage, and networking resources across distributed locations. By leveraging distributed edge computing architectures, organizations can build scalable, resilient, and efficient edge computing solutions that meet the diverse requirements of modern applications and services. In summary, taxonomy of edge computing architectures provides a framework for understanding the various approaches and configurations used in deploying distributed computing systems at the network edge. By classifying edge computing architectures based on factors such as topology, hierarchy, resource allocation, and data processing models, organizations can design, deploy, and manage edge computing solutions that meet their specific needs and requirements.

Chapter 2: Design Principles for Edge Computing

Efficient edge computing design hinges on several fundamental principles that enable organizations to maximize the performance, scalability, and reliability of their distributed computing systems at the network edge. CLI commands such as Docker or Kubernetes can be used to deploy containerized applications that run on edge nodes, ensuring consistency and scalability across distributed environments. One core principle of efficient edge computing design is resource optimization, which involves maximizing the utilization of computing, storage, and networking resources while minimizing waste and inefficiencies.

CLI commands such as top or htop can be used to monitor resource utilization metrics such as CPU usage, memory usage, and disk I/O on edge nodes, identifying resource-intensive processes and potential performance bottlenecks. By optimizing resource allocation and management, organizations can ensure that edge computing systems operate efficiently and cost-effectively. Another key principle of efficient edge computing design is fault tolerance, which involves designing systems that can continue to operate reliably in the presence of failures or disruptions. CLI commands such as Ansible or Terraform can be used to automate the deployment and provisioning of edge devices, ensuring consistency and scalability across distributed environments. By deploying redundant components, implementing error detection and recovery mechanisms, and leveraging distributed consensus protocols, organizations can build resilient edge computing systems that can withstand hardware failures, network outages, and other disruptions. Scalability is another critical principle of efficient edge computing design, which involves designing systems that can accommodate growth in data volume, user traffic, and application complexity over time.

CLI commands such as Kubernetes or Docker Swarm can be used to deploy containerized applications that can scale dynamically based on demand, ensuring that edge computing systems can handle increasing workloads and user traffic without sacrificing performance or reliability. By designing systems with horizontal scalability in mind, organizations can add or remove edge nodes and resources as needed, enabling them to adapt to changing business requirements and user needs. Efficiency is a core principle of edge computing design, which involves optimizing the performance, energy consumption, and cost-effectiveness of computing systems at the network edge. CLI commands such as nmap or netstat can be used to scan for open ports and identify potential security vulnerabilities in edge devices and nodes. By optimizing algorithms, data structures, and software architectures, organizations can minimize the computational and energy requirements of edge computing applications, reducing operating costs and environmental impact.

Additionally, organizations can leverage techniques such as data compression, deduplication, and caching to minimize the amount of data transmitted over the network and stored on edge devices, further improving efficiency and reducing resource usage. Security is a foundational principle of efficient edge computing design, which involves protecting sensitive data, preventing unauthorized access, and ensuring the integrity, confidentiality, and availability of computing systems at the network edge. CLI commands such as SSH or SCP can be used to remotely access edge nodes and deploy *applications or updates, ensuring seamless integration with edge computing systems. By implementing encryption, authentication, access control, and intrusion detection measures, organizations can safeguard edge computing systems against cyber threats, ensuring that sensitive data and critical infrastructure remain protected from unauthorized access and malicious attacks. Finally, simplicity is a guiding principle of efficient edge computing design, which involves minimizing complexity, reducing dependencies, and streamlining operations to improve usability, maintainability, and agility. CLI commands such as lspci or lscpu can be used to view hardware specifications and identify compatible hardware components for edge computing deployments. By adopting modular architectures, standardized interfaces, and automated management tools, organizations can simplify the deployment, configuration, and maintenance of edge computing systems, enabling them to focus on innovation and value creation rather than infrastructure management. In summary, principles of efficient edge computing design encompass resource optimization, fault tolerance, scalability, efficiency, security, and simplicity, enabling organizations to build resilient, scalable, cost-effective, and user-friendly distributed* computing systems at the network edge. By adhering to these principles, organizations can unlock the full potential of edge computing and drive innovation in diverse industries and sectors. Design patterns and strategies play a crucial role in architecting efficient and scalable edge computing environments, enabling organizations to address the unique challenges and requirements of distributed computing at the network edge. CLI commands such as Docker or Kubernetes can be used to deploy containerized applications that run on edge nodes, ensuring consistency and scalability across distributed environments. One design pattern commonly used in edge environments is the microservices architecture, which involves decomposing applications into smaller, loosely coupled services that can be independently deployed, scaled, and managed.

CLI commands such as Ansible or Terraform can be used to automate the deployment and provisioning of edge devices, ensuring consistency and scalability across distributed environments. By adopting a microservices architecture, organizations can improve agility, scalability, and fault tolerance, enabling them to develop and deploy edge applications more efficiently and *effectively. Another design pattern for edge environments is the use of serverless computing, which involves running code in response to events without the need to provision or manage servers. CLI commands such as AWS CLI or Azure CLI can be used to interact with edge computing platforms and cloud services, enabling organizations to build hybrid edge-cloud architectures that leverage the scalability and flexibility of the cloud while harnessing the low latency and data locality benefits of edge computing. By leveraging serverless computing, organizations can reduce operational overhead, improve resource utilization, and scale applications dynamically based on demand, enabling them to deliver real-time insights and experiences to end-users at the network edge. Edge caching is another design pattern used in edge environments, which involves storing frequently accessed data closer to end-users and devices to reduce latency and improve performance. CLI commands such as scp or rsync can be used to transfer data between edge nodes and centralized servers, ensuring that data is cached and updated efficiently. By caching data at the network edge, organizations can minimize the amount of data transmitted over the network, reduce bandwidth usage, and improve the responsiveness of edge applications, enabling* them to deliver faster and more seamless user experiences. Additionally, edge caching can help organizations mitigate the impact of network outages or disruptions by ensuring that critical data and content remain accessible even when connectivity to centralized servers is lost. Edge orchestration is another design pattern used in edge environments, which involves automating the deployment, configuration, and management of edge nodes and applications. CLI commands such as SSH or SCP can be used to remotely access edge nodes and deploy applications or updates, ensuring seamless integration with edge computing systems.

By adopting edge orchestration, organizations can streamline the provisioning and lifecycle management of edge nodes, improve resource utilization, and reduce operational complexity, enabling them to scale their edge computing deployments more efficiently and effectively. Additionally, edge orchestration can help organizations enforce security policies, ensure compliance, and maintain consistency across distributed environments, enabling them to mitigate risks and vulnerabilities associated with edge computing. In summary, design patterns and strategies are essential for architecting efficient *and scalable edge computing environments, enabling organizations to address the unique challenges and requirements of distributed computing at the network edge. By leveraging microservices architecture, serverless computing, edge caching, and edge orchestration, organizations can build resilient, scalable, and high-performance edge computing solutions that deliver real-time insights and experiences to end-users and devices at the network edge.*

Chapter 3: Scalable Infrastructure Design

Scalability considerations are paramount in the design and implementation of edge infrastructure, ensuring that systems can handle increasing workloads and user demands as they grow over time. CLI commands such as Docker or Kubernetes can be used to deploy containerized applications that run on edge nodes, ensuring consistency and scalability across distributed environments. One key aspect of scalability in edge infrastructure is the ability to scale computing resources dynamically based on demand, enabling organizations to accommodate fluctuations in workload and user traffic without sacrificing performance or reliability. CLI commands such as Ansible or Terraform can be used to automate the deployment and provisioning of edge devices, ensuring consistency and scalability across distributed environments. By leveraging automation and orchestration tools, organizations can deploy new edge nodes, scale resources up or down, and manage configurations efficiently, enabling them to adapt to changing business requirements and user needs. Additionally, organizations can leverage techniques such as auto-scaling and load balancing to distribute workloads evenly across edge nodes and ensure optimal resource utilization. CLI commands such as AWS CLI or Azure CLI can be used to interact with edge computing platforms and cloud services, enabling organizations to build hybrid edge-cloud architectures that leverage the scalability and flexibility of the cloud while harnessing the low latency and data locality benefits of edge computing. Another consideration in edge infrastructure scalability is the ability to scale storage capacity to accommodate growing volumes of data generated by edge devices and applications. CLI commands such as scp or rsync can be used to transfer data between edge nodes and centralized servers, ensuring that data is replicated and synchronized efficiently. By adopting distributed storage solutions and data replication techniques, organizations can ensure data availability, durability, and consistency across distributed environments, enabling them to store and access large volumes of data at the network edge. Network scalability is also critical in edge infrastructure, ensuring that networks can accommodate increasing numbers of edge devices and nodes while maintaining performance and reliability. CLI commands such as ping or traceroute can be used to measure network latency and identify potential bottlenecks in the communication path between edge devices and backend servers. By deploying scalable network architectures such as mesh networks or edge fabrics, organizations can distribute network traffic evenly, optimize bandwidth usage, and improve resilience and fault tolerance, enabling them to deliver consistent and reliable connectivity to end-users and devices at the network edge. Additionally, organizations can leverage technologies such as network function virtualization (NFV) and software-defined networking (SDN) to abstract network functions and policies from underlying hardware, enabling them to scale networks dynamically and adapt to changing traffic patterns and requirements. Security scalability is another consideration in edge infrastructure, ensuring that security measures can scale to protect against evolving cyber threats and vulnerabilities. CLI commands such as SSH or SCP can be used to remotely access edge nodes and deploy applications or updates, ensuring seamless integration with edge computing systems. By adopting a layered approach to security and implementing security measures such as encryption, authentication, access control, and intrusion detection, organizations can mitigate risks and vulnerabilities associated with edge computing, ensuring the integrity, confidentiality, and availability of data and systems at the network edge. In summary, scalability considerations are essential in the design and implementation of edge infrastructure, enabling organizations to accommodate growing workloads, data volumes, and user demands while maintaining performance, reliability, and security. By adopting scalable computing, storage, network, and security solutions, organizations can build resilient, high-performance edge computing environments that deliver real-time insights and experiences to end-users and devices at the network edge.

Designing for scalability in edge computing systems is essential to ensure that distributed architectures can handle growing workloads and user demands as they evolve over time. CLI commands such as Docker or Kubernetes can be used to deploy containerized applications that run on edge nodes, ensuring consistency and scalability across distributed environments. One key aspect of designing for scalability in edge computing systems is adopting a modular and flexible architecture that can scale horizontally to accommodate increasing computational and storage requirements. CLI commands such as Ansible or Terraform can be used to automate the deployment and provisioning of edge devices, ensuring consistency and scalability across distributed environments. By breaking down applications into smaller, independently deployable components, organizations can scale individual services or functions based on demand, enabling them to allocate resources efficiently and adapt to changing workload patterns. Additionally, organizations can leverage techniques such as load balancing and auto-scaling to distribute workloads evenly across edge nodes and ensure optimal resource utilization. CLI commands such as AWS CLI or Azure CLI can be used to interact with edge computing platforms and cloud services, enabling organizations to build hybrid edge-cloud architectures that leverage the scalability and flexibility of the cloud while harnessing the low latency and data locality benefits of edge computing. Another aspect of designing for scalability in edge computing systems is optimizing data management and storage to handle growing volumes of data generated by edge devices and applications. CLI commands such as scp or rsync can be used to transfer data between edge nodes and centralized servers, ensuring that data is replicated and synchronized efficiently. By adopting distributed storage solutions and data replication techniques, *organizations can ensure data availability, durability, and consistency across distributed environments, enabling them to store and access large volumes of data at the network edge. Network scalability is also critical in edge computing systems, ensuring that networks can accommodate increasing numbers of edge devices and nodes while maintaining performance and reliability. CLI commands such as ping or traceroute can be used to measure network latency and identify potential bottlenecks in the communication path between edge devices and backend servers. By deploying scalable network architectures such as mesh networks or edge fabrics, organizations can distribute network traffic evenly, optimize bandwidth usage, and improve resilience and fault tolerance, enabling them to deliver consistent and reliable connectivity to end-users and devices at the network edge. Additionally, organizations can leverage technologies such as network function virtualization (NFV) and software-defined networking (SDN) to abstract network functions and policies from underlying hardware, enabling them to scale networks dynamically and adapt to changing traffic patterns and requirements. Security scalability is another consideration in edge computing systems, ensuring that security* measures can scale to protect against evolving cyber threats and vulnerabilities. CLI commands such as SSH or SCP can be used to remotely access edge nodes and deploy applications or updates, ensuring seamless integration with edge computing systems. By adopting a layered approach to security and implementing security measures such as encryption, authentication, access control, and intrusion detection, organizations can mitigate risks and vulnerabilities associated with edge computing, ensuring the integrity, confidentiality, and availability of data and systems at the network edge. In summary, designing for scalability in edge computing systems is essential to ensure that distributed architectures can accommodate growing workloads, data volumes, and user demands while maintaining performance, reliability, and security. By adopting scalable computing, storage, network, and security solutions, organizations can build resilient, high-performance edge computing environments that deliver real-time insights and experiences to end-users and devices at the network edge.

Chapter 4: Network Design and Optimization

Network topologies are critical elements in the design and implementation of edge computing systems, providing the framework for how devices and resources are interconnected and communicate within the network. CLI commands such as traceroute or ping can be used to measure network latency and identify potential bottlenecks in the communication path between edge devices and backend servers. One common network topology used in edge computing is the star topology, where edge devices are connected directly to a central hub or switch, enabling efficient communication and data transfer between devices and centralized resources. CLI commands such as ifconfig or ip can be used to view network interfaces and configure IP addresses on edge devices, ensuring connectivity and interoperability within the network. The star topology is well-suited for small-scale edge deployments where devices are located in close proximity to each other and require low-latency communication with centralized servers or cloud resources. Another network topology used in edge computing is the mesh topology, where edge devices are interconnected with each other in a decentralized manner, forming a network of interconnected nodes that can communicate directly with each other. CLI commands such as ARP or netstat can be used to view network routing tables and identify the paths that data takes through the network, ensuring efficient routing and data transmission. The mesh topology is well-suited for large-scale edge deployments where devices are spread out across a wide geographic area and need to communicate with each other over long distances. By leveraging the mesh topology, organizations can build resilient and fault-tolerant edge networks that can adapt to changing conditions and route traffic dynamically based on network conditions and availability. A hybrid topology, combining elements of both star and mesh topologies, is also commonly used in edge computing deployments to balance the benefits of centralized control and decentralized communication. CLI commands such as route or ip route can be used to configure network routing tables and specify how data should be routed between different network segments, ensuring efficient communication and data transfer within the network. In a hybrid topology, edge devices may be connected to a central hub or switch for communication with centralized resources while also maintaining direct connections with neighboring devices for local communication and data exchange. This approach enables organizations to leverage the benefits of both centralized and decentralized communication, optimizing network performance and scalability for edge computing applications. Additionally, organizations can deploy edge computing gateways or routers at the network edge to aggregate and process data locally before forwarding it to centralized servers or cloud resources, reducing latency and bandwidth usage for edge applications. CLI commands such as iptables or firewalld can be used to configure firewall rules and security policies on edge devices and gateways, ensuring that sensitive data and critical infrastructure remain protected from unauthorized access and malicious attacks. In summary, network topologies play a crucial role in the design and implementation of edge computing systems, providing the foundation for how devices and resources are interconnected and communicate within the network. By selecting the appropriate network topology based on the specific requirements and constraints of their deployment, organizations can build resilient, scalable, and efficient edge computing networks that deliver real-time insights and experiences to end-users and devices at the network edge.

Optimization techniques are essential for enhancing the performance and efficiency of edge networks, ensuring that they can deliver fast, reliable, and responsive connectivity to end-users and devices at the network edge. CLI commands such as traceroute or ping can be used to measure network latency and identify potential bottlenecks in the communication path between edge devices and backend servers. One optimization technique for improving edge network performance is the use of content delivery networks (CDNs), which cache content closer to end-users and devices to reduce latency and improve responsiveness. CLI commands such as dig or nslookup can be used to query DNS servers and resolve domain names to IP addresses, ensuring that content is delivered from the nearest edge server or cache to minimize latency and improve user experience. By distributing content across multiple edge locations, CDNs can reduce the distance that data needs to travel over the network, improving throughput and reducing the risk of congestion and packet loss. Another optimization technique for edge network performance is the use of traffic shaping and prioritization to prioritize critical traffic and ensure that it receives preferential treatment over less important traffic. CLI commands such as tc or iptables can be used to configure traffic shaping rules and quality of service (QoS) policies on edge devices and routers, ensuring that bandwidth is allocated efficiently and fairly across different types of traffic. By prioritizing real-time and latency-sensitive applications such as voice and video conferencing, organizations can ensure that they receive sufficient bandwidth and low-latency connectivity, enabling them to deliver seamless and responsive user experiences at the network edge. Additionally, organizations can leverage techniques such as protocol optimization and compression to reduce the size of data packets transmitted over the network, improving throughput and reducing latency for edge applications. CLI commands such as gzip or brotli can be used to compress data before transmission, reducing bandwidth usage and improving network performance for edge applications. By optimizing protocols such as TCP/IP and HTTP/HTTPS, organizations can minimize overhead and latency associated with protocol handshakes and data transmission, enabling them to deliver faster and more efficient communication between edge devices and backend servers. Edge caching is another optimization technique used to improve network performance by storing frequently accessed data closer to end-users and devices, reducing latency and improving responsiveness for edge applications. CLI commands such as scp or rsync can be used to transfer data between edge nodes and centralized servers, ensuring that data is cached and updated efficiently. By caching data at the network edge, organizations can minimize the amount of data transmitted over the network, reduce bandwidth usage, and improve the responsiveness of edge applications, enabling them to deliver faster and more seamless user experiences. Additionally, edge caching can help organizations mitigate the impact of network outages or disruptions by ensuring that critical data and content remain accessible even when connectivity to centralized servers is lost. Network optimization is a continuous process that requires monitoring, analysis, and adjustment to ensure that edge networks perform optimally under changing conditions and workloads. CLI commands such as iftop or iptraf can be used to monitor network traffic and performance metrics in real-time, enabling organizations to identify potential bottlenecks and performance issues before they impact users and applications. By analyzing network traffic patterns and performance metrics, organizations can identify opportunities for optimization and implement changes to improve network performance and efficiency. In summary, optimization techniques such as CDN deployment, traffic shaping, protocol optimization, compression, and edge caching are essential for improving the performance and efficiency of edge networks, enabling organizations to deliver fast, reliable, and responsive connectivity to end-users and devices at the network edge. By leveraging these techniques, organizations can minimize latency, reduce bandwidth usage, and improve user experience for edge applications, ensuring that they can meet the demands of modern digital businesses and deliver value to customers in real-time.

Chapter 5: Data Storage and Management Strategies

Data storage models in edge computing play a pivotal role in facilitating efficient and reliable storage of data generated by edge devices and applications, ensuring that data is accessible, secure, and scalable at the network edge. CLI commands such as df or du can be used to check disk space usage and identify storage capacity on edge devices, enabling organizations to manage storage resources effectively. One commonly used data storage model in edge computing is distributed storage, where data is replicated and distributed across multiple edge nodes to ensure redundancy, availability, and fault tolerance. CLI commands such as scp or rsync can be used to transfer data between edge nodes and centralized servers, ensuring that data is replicated and synchronized efficiently. By leveraging distributed storage solutions such as HDFS (Hadoop Distributed File System) or Ceph, organizations can ensure data availability and durability across distributed environments, enabling them to store and access large volumes of data at the network edge. Another data storage model in edge computing is fog storage, which involves storing data in close proximity to edge devices and applications to minimize latency and improve responsiveness. CLI commands such as mount or fstab can be used to mount remote storage volumes or file systems on edge devices, enabling them to access data stored in centralized repositories or cloud storage services. By deploying edge caching and storage solutions such as Redis or Memcached, organizations can cache frequently accessed data locally on edge devices, reducing the need to retrieve data from centralized repositories and improving application performance. Additionally, organizations can leverage techniques such as data deduplication and compression to minimize the amount of data transmitted over the network and stored on edge devices, further improving efficiency and reducing resource usage. Edge computing platforms and cloud services offer various storage options and services that organizations can leverage to build scalable and resilient data storage solutions at the network edge. CLI commands such as AWS CLI or Azure CLI can be used to interact with edge computing platforms and cloud storage services, enabling organizations to provision, configure, and manage storage resources dynamically. By leveraging cloud storage services such as Amazon

S3 or Azure Blob Storage, organizations can offload data storage and management tasks to the cloud, reducing the need for on-premises infrastructure and overhead. Additionally, organizations can deploy edge computing gateways or routers with built-in storage capabilities to aggregate and process data locally before forwarding it to centralized repositories or cloud storage services. This approach reduces latency and bandwidth usage for edge applications while ensuring that data remains accessible and secure at the network edge. Security is a critical consideration in data storage models for edge computing, ensuring that sensitive data and critical infrastructure remain protected from unauthorized access and malicious attacks. CLI commands such as chmod or chown can be used to set permissions and ownership on files and directories, ensuring that only authorized users and applications have access to sensitive data. By encrypting data at rest and in transit, organizations can safeguard data against unauthorized access and interception, ensuring the integrity, confidentiality, and availability of data stored in edge computing environments. Additionally, organizations can implement access control policies and authentication mechanisms to verify the identity of users and devices accessing data stored in edge computing environments, mitigating risks and vulnerabilities associated with data storage and management. In summary, data storage models in edge computing play a crucial role in ensuring efficient, reliable, and secure storage of data generated by edge devices and applications. By leveraging distributed storage, fog storage, cloud storage services, and security best practices, organizations can build scalable, resilient, and cost-effective data storage solutions at the network edge, enabling them to unlock the full potential of edge computing and deliver value to customers in real-time. Management strategies for edge data storage are essential for ensuring efficient, reliable, and secure storage of data generated by edge devices and applications, enabling organizations to maximize the value of their edge computing deployments. CLI commands such as df or du can be used to check disk space usage and identify storage capacity on edge devices, enabling organizations to manage storage resources effectively. One key management strategy for edge data storage is data lifecycle management, which involves defining policies and procedures for storing, archiving, and deleting data based on its value, relevance, and regulatory requirements. CLI commands such as find or rm can be used to search for and delete files or directories that meet specific criteria, ensuring that data is managed and disposed of in accordance with organizational policies and legal obligations. By implementing data lifecycle management practices, organizations can optimize storage resources, reduce costs, and mitigate risks associated with storing large volumes of data at the network edge. Another management strategy for edge data storage is data deduplication and compression, which involves identifying and eliminating redundant or duplicate data and compressing data to reduce storage space and bandwidth usage. CLI commands such as tar or gzip can be used to compress files or directories before storing them on edge devices, reducing storage requirements and improving efficiency. By deduplicating and compressing data, organizations can optimize storage utilization, improve performance, and reduce the cost of storing and transmitting data over the network. Additionally, organizations can leverage techniques such as tiered storage and caching to optimize data access and retrieval in edge computing environments. CLI commands such as mount or fstab can be used to mount remote storage volumes or file systems on edge devices, enabling them to access data stored in centralized *repositories or cloud storage services. By deploying edge caching and storage solutions such as Redis or Memcached, organizations can cache frequently accessed data locally on edge devices, reducing the need to retrieve data from centralized repositories and improving application performance. Another management strategy for edge data storage is data replication and synchronization, which involves replicating data across multiple edge nodes to ensure redundancy, availability, and fault tolerance. CLI commands such as rsync or scp can be used to transfer data between edge nodes and centralized servers, ensuring that data is replicated and synchronized efficiently. By leveraging distributed storage solutions such as HDFS (Hadoop Distributed File System) or Ceph, organizations can ensure data availability and durability across distributed environments, enabling them to store and access large volumes of data at the network edge. Security is a critical consideration in data storage management for edge computing, ensuring that sensitive data and critical infrastructure remain protected from unauthorized access and malicious attacks. CLI commands such as chmod or chown can be used to set permissions and ownership on files and directories, ensuring that only authorized users and applications have access to sensitive* data. By encrypting data at rest and in transit, organizations can safeguard data against unauthorized access and interception, ensuring the integrity, confidentiality, and availability of data stored in edge computing environments. Additionally, organizations can implement access control policies and authentication mechanisms to verify the identity of users and devices accessing data stored in edge computing environments, mitigating risks and vulnerabilities associated with data storage and management. In summary, management strategies for edge data storage are essential for ensuring efficient, reliable, and secure storage of data generated by edge devices and applications. By implementing data lifecycle management, deduplication and compression, replication and synchronization, and security best practices, organizations can build scalable, resilient, and cost-effective data storage solutions at the network edge, enabling them to unlock the full potential of edge computing and deliver value to customers in real-time.

Chapter 6: Edge Device Selection and Configuration

Selecting edge devices involves careful consideration of various criteria to ensure that they meet the specific requirements and constraints of edge computing deployments, enabling organizations to build scalable, efficient, and reliable edge computing environments. CLI commands such as lspci or lshw can be used to view hardware information and specifications on edge devices, enabling organizations to assess their capabilities and compatibility with edge computing workloads. One key criterion for selecting edge devices is performance, which involves evaluating the processing power, memory, and storage capacity of devices to ensure that they can handle the computational and storage requirements of edge applications. CLI commands such as top or htop can be used to monitor CPU and memory usage on edge devices, enabling organizations to assess their performance under different workloads and conditions. By selecting edge devices with sufficient processing power and memory, organizations can ensure that they can run edge applications efficiently and deliver fast, responsive *user experiences at the network edge. Another criterion for selecting edge devices is connectivity, which involves evaluating the network interfaces and communication capabilities of devices to ensure that they can connect to other devices and resources in the edge computing environment. CLI commands such as ifconfig or ip can be used to configure network interfaces and view network connectivity status on edge devices, enabling organizations to assess their compatibility with existing network infrastructure and protocols. By selecting edge devices with wired or wireless connectivity options such as Ethernet, Wi-Fi, or cellular, organizations can ensure that they can communicate with other devices and access centralized resources effectively, enabling them to build interconnected and interoperable edge computing environments. Additionally, organizations can leverage techniques such as network bonding or link aggregation to increase network bandwidth and reliability for edge devices, ensuring that they can handle high volumes of data traffic and maintain connectivity in challenging network conditions. Power efficiency is another important criterion for selecting edge devices, especially in remote or resource-constrained environments where access to power sources may be limited or unreliable. CLI* commands such as powertop or acpi can be used to monitor power usage and optimize power settings on edge devices, enabling organizations to maximize energy efficiency and prolong battery life in battery-powered devices. By selecting edge devices with low power consumption and efficient power management features, organizations can minimize operating costs and environmental impact while ensuring continuous operation in off-grid or environmentally sensitive locations. Another criterion for selecting edge devices is ruggedness and durability, which involves evaluating the physical design, construction, and environmental specifications of devices to ensure that they can withstand harsh operating conditions and environments. CLI commands such as smartctl or hdparm can be used to check disk health and monitor hardware reliability on edge devices, enabling organizations to assess their robustness and resilience under different environmental stressors and factors. By selecting edge devices with ruggedized enclosures, sealed connectors, and wide temperature ranges, organizations can ensure that they can operate reliably in extreme temperatures, humidity levels, vibration, and shock, enabling them to deploy edge computing solutions in industrial, outdoor, or mission-critical applications with confidence.

Security is another critical criterion for selecting edge devices, ensuring that sensitive data and critical infrastructure remain protected from unauthorized access and malicious attacks. CLI commands such as iptables or firewalld can be used to configure firewall rules and security policies on edge devices, enabling organizations to control access to network services and ports and mitigate risks associated with network security threats and vulnerabilities. By selecting edge devices with built-in security features such as hardware-based encryption, secure boot, and trusted platform modules (TPM), organizations can enhance the security posture of their edge computing deployments and safeguard sensitive data and critical infrastructure from unauthorized access and tampering. In summary, selecting edge devices involves evaluating various criteria such as performance, connectivity, power efficiency, ruggedness, and security to ensure that they meet the specific requirements and constraints of edge computing deployments. By carefully considering these criteria and selecting devices that align with their goals and objectives, organizations can build scalable, efficient, and reliable edge computing environments that deliver value to customers in real-time.

Configuration best practices for edge devices are

crucial for ensuring their optimal performance, security, and reliability in edge computing environments, enabling organizations to effectively deploy and manage their edge infrastructure. CLI commands such as ifconfig or ip can be used to configure network interfaces and IP addresses on edge devices, enabling organizations to establish connectivity and communication within their edge networks. One key aspect of configuration best practices is standardization, which involves defining and enforcing consistent configuration settings across all edge devices to simplify management and troubleshooting. CLI commands such as ansible or puppet can be used to automate configuration management tasks and apply standardized configuration templates to multiple edge devices simultaneously, ensuring consistency and compliance with organizational policies and standards. By standardizing configuration settings such as network parameters, security policies, and system settings, organizations can reduce the risk of misconfiguration errors and minimize the time and effort required to deploy and maintain their edge infrastructure. Another best practice for configuring edge devices is to implement security measures such as access control, authentication, and encryption to protect sensitive data and infrastructure from unauthorized access and malicious attacks. CLI commands such as ssh-keygen or openssl can be used to generate SSH keys and SSL/TLS certificates for secure communication and authentication between edge devices and backend servers, ensuring that only authorized users and devices can access and interact with sensitive data and resources. By implementing strong access control policies and encryption mechanisms, organizations can mitigate risks associated with data breaches, unauthorized access, and data interception, ensuring the confidentiality, integrity, and availability of data stored and processed on edge devices. Additionally, organizations should regularly update and patch firmware, operating systems, and software applications on edge devices to address security vulnerabilities and ensure that they are protected against emerging threats and exploits. CLI commands such as apt or yum can be used to install updates and patches on edge devices, ensuring that they have the latest security fixes and performance enhancements applied. By staying up-to-date with software updates and security patches, organizations can reduce the risk of security incidents and ensure the stability and reliability of their edge infrastructure. Configuration backups are another important best practice for edge devices, enabling organizations to restore device configurations in the event of configuration errors, hardware failures, or security breaches. CLI commands such as rsync or scp can be used to backup configuration files and settings to remote servers or cloud storage services, ensuring that they are safely stored and accessible for recovery purposes. By regularly backing up device configurations and settings, organizations can minimize downtime and data loss in the event of unexpected incidents or disasters, ensuring business continuity and operational resilience for their edge infrastructure. Documentation and documentation management are essential components of configuration best practices for edge devices, enabling organizations to maintain accurate records of device configurations, changes, and deployments for auditing, compliance, and troubleshooting purposes. CLI commands such as git or svn can be used to version control configuration files and documentation, enabling organizations to track changes and collaborate on configuration management tasks effectively. By documenting configuration settings, dependencies, and procedures, organizations can streamline troubleshooting and knowledge transfer, empower IT staff to make informed decisions, and *ensure that configuration changes are performed safely and efficiently. In summary, configuration best practices for edge devices are essential for ensuring their optimal performance, security, and reliability in edge computing environments. By standardizing configuration settings, implementing security measures, applying software updates, backing up configurations, and documenting configurations and procedures, organizations can build and maintain robust and resilient edge infrastructure that meets their business needs and objectives.*

Chapter 7: Application Design for Edge Environments

Principles of edge application design are fundamental for creating efficient, scalable, and responsive applications tailored to the unique challenges and opportunities presented by edge computing environments. CLI commands such as docker or kubectl can be used to deploy and manage containerized applications on edge devices, enabling organizations to encapsulate and isolate application components for efficient deployment and operation. One key principle of edge application design is modularity, which involves breaking down complex applications into smaller, self-contained modules or microservices that can be independently developed, deployed, and scaled. By modularizing applications, organizations can improve agility, flexibility, and maintainability, enabling them to quickly adapt to changing business requirements and market demands. CLI commands such as git or svn can be used to version control application code and manage dependencies, enabling organizations to track changes and collaborate on application development effectively. By adopting a modular *architecture, organizations can streamline development, deployment, and maintenance processes, accelerate time-to-market, and reduce the risk of application failures and downtime. Another principle of edge application design is latency awareness, which involves optimizing application design and architecture to minimize latency and improve responsiveness for edge applications. CLI commands such as traceroute or ping can be used to measure network latency and identify potential bottlenecks in the communication path between edge devices and backend servers, enabling organizations to optimize application performance and user experience. By leveraging techniques such as edge caching, pre-fetching, and local processing, organizations can reduce the round-trip time for data transmission and processing, ensuring that edge applications deliver fast, seamless, and interactive user experiences. Additionally, organizations can leverage edge analytics and machine learning algorithms to analyze and process data locally on edge devices, enabling them to derive real-time insights and make timely decisions without relying on centralized servers or cloud resources. Scalability is another critical principle of edge application design, ensuring that applications can handle increasing workloads and user demands without compromising performance or reliability. CLI commands such as docker-compose or kubernetes can be used to orchestrate and manage application containers across multiple edge devices, enabling organizations to scale applications horizontally or vertically to meet changing demand. By designing applications with scalability in mind, organizations can ensure that they can dynamically allocate resources, distribute workloads, and handle peak traffic efficiently, enabling them to deliver consistent performance and quality of service for edge applications. Resilience and fault tolerance are essential principles of edge application design, ensuring that applications can withstand failures and disruptions in edge computing environments. CLI commands such as systemctl or service can be used to monitor and manage application services and processes on edge devices, enabling organizations to detect and recover from failures quickly. By implementing redundant components, distributed architectures, and automated failover mechanisms, organizations can ensure that applications remain available and responsive even in the face of hardware failures, network outages, or software bugs. Additionally, organizations can leverage techniques such as circuit breakers, retries, and graceful degradation to handle errors* and mitigate the impact of failures on application performance and user experience. Security is a fundamental principle of edge application design, ensuring that applications and data remain protected from unauthorized access, tampering, and exploitation. CLI commands such as iptables or firewalld can be used to configure firewall rules and security policies on edge devices, enabling organizations to control access to network services and ports and prevent malicious attacks. By implementing encryption, authentication, and access control mechanisms, organizations can safeguard data and applications from threats such as eavesdropping, interception, and data breaches. Additionally, organizations should regularly update and patch application dependencies and libraries to address security vulnerabilities and ensure that applications remain secure and compliant with industry regulations and standards. In summary, principles of edge application design are essential for creating efficient, scalable, and resilient applications that can meet the demands of edge computing environments. By embracing modularity, latency awareness, scalability, resilience, and security, organizations can design and deploy edge applications that deliver value to customers in real-time, enable innovative use cases, and drive *business growth and competitiveness in the digital era.*

Developing and deploying applications for edge computing requires careful consideration of various factors and best practices to ensure that they are efficient, reliable, and scalable in edge environments. CLI commands such as git or svn can be used to version control application code and manage collaboration among developers, enabling organizations to track changes and maintain code quality throughout the development lifecycle. One key aspect of developing applications for edge computing is understanding the unique characteristics and constraints of edge environments, such as limited compute resources, intermittent connectivity, and stringent latency requirements. By designing applications with these considerations in mind, organizations can ensure that they can operate effectively in edge environments and deliver value to end-users in real-time. CLI commands such as docker or kubernetes can be used to containerize and orchestrate applications for deployment in edge environments, enabling organizations to encapsulate application components and dependencies and manage them efficiently across distributed infrastructure. Containerization simplifies application deployment and management by providing a lightweight, portable runtime environment that isolates applications from underlying infrastructure dependencies, ensuring consistency and reliability across different deployment environments. Another important consideration in developing applications for edge computing is optimizing performance and resource utilization to maximize efficiency and responsiveness. CLI commands such as top or htop can be used to monitor resource usage and performance metrics on edge devices, enabling organizations to identify bottlenecks and optimize application code and configurations accordingly. By minimizing resource consumption and optimizing application code for performance, organizations can ensure that applications can operate efficiently in resource-constrained edge environments and deliver fast, responsive user experiences. Additionally, organizations should leverage techniques such as edge caching, pre-fetching, and local processing to minimize latency and improve responsiveness for edge applications. Edge caching involves storing frequently accessed data locally on edge devices to reduce the round-trip time for data transmission and processing, enabling applications to respond quickly to user requests and deliver seamless user experiences. Pre-fetching involves predicting user behavior and pre-loading data or content onto edge devices before it is requested, further reducing latency and improving application performance. Local processing involves offloading computational tasks and analytics to edge devices, enabling applications to derive real-time insights and make timely decisions without relying on centralized servers or cloud resources. Security is another critical consideration in developing applications for edge computing, ensuring that applications and data remain protected from unauthorized access, tampering, and exploitation. CLI commands such as iptables or firewalld can be used to configure firewall rules and security policies on edge devices, enabling organizations to control access to network services and ports and prevent malicious attacks. By implementing encryption, authentication, and access control mechanisms, organizations can safeguard data and applications from threats such as eavesdropping, interception, and data breaches. Additionally, organizations should regularly update and patch application dependencies and libraries to address security vulnerabilities and ensure that applications remain secure and compliant with industry regulations and standards. In summary, developing and deploying applications for edge computing requires a holistic *approach that considers various factors such as application architecture, performance optimization, security, and scalability. By embracing containerization, performance optimization, edge caching, and security best practices, organizations can design and deploy edge applications that deliver value to customers in real-time, enable innovative use cases, and drive business growth and competitiveness in the digital era.*

Chapter 8: Security Architecture and Best Practices

Security challenges in edge environments present unique complexities and risks that organizations must address to safeguard sensitive data, protect critical infrastructure, and mitigate the impact of cyber threats. CLI commands such as nmap or netstat can be used to scan for open ports and network vulnerabilities on edge devices, enabling organizations to assess their security posture and identify potential weaknesses or gaps in their defenses. One of the primary security challenges in edge environments is the distributed nature of edge computing architecture, which involves deploying computing resources and processing data at the network edge, closer to where data is generated and consumed. This distributed architecture introduces new attack vectors and vulnerabilities, as edge devices may lack the robust security controls and protections typically found in centralized data centers or cloud environments. CLI commands such as ssh or scp can be used to securely access and transfer files between edge devices and backend servers, enabling organizations to manage and monitor edge devices remotely while minimizing the risk of unauthorized access or data breaches. Another security challenge in edge environments is the limited resources and capabilities of edge devices, which may lack the processing power, memory, and storage capacity to implement robust security measures or run comprehensive security software. CLI commands such as top or ps can be used to monitor system processes and resource usage on edge devices, enabling organizations to identify and mitigate security threats and performance issues in real-time. By implementing lightweight security solutions and adopting a defense-in-depth approach, organizations can strengthen the security posture of edge devices and protect them from common threats such as malware, ransomware, and unauthorized access. Additionally, organizations should leverage techniques such as network segmentation, isolation, and encryption to compartmentalize and protect sensitive data and applications running on edge devices. Network segmentation involves dividing the network into separate subnets or VLANs based on security requirements and access controls, limiting the scope of potential attacks and minimizing the impact of security breaches. CLI commands such as iptables or firewalld can be used to configure firewall rules and access control lists (ACLs) on edge devices, enabling organizations to control traffic flow and prevent unauthorized access to sensitive data and resources. Isolation involves isolating edge devices and applications from each other and from external networks to prevent lateral movement and limit the propagation of malware and other security threats. By isolating edge devices and enforcing strict access controls, organizations can minimize the risk of unauthorized access and data exfiltration, ensuring the integrity and confidentiality of data stored and processed on edge devices. Encryption is another essential security measure for protecting data in transit and at rest in edge environments, ensuring that sensitive information remains confidential and secure from interception or tampering. CLI commands such as openssl or gpg can be used to generate and manage encryption keys and certificates for securing communications and data storage on edge devices, enabling organizations to establish secure channels and protect sensitive data from unauthorized access or disclosure. By encrypting data using strong cryptographic algorithms and enforcing encryption policies and standards, organizations can ensure that data remains protected from unauthorized access and exploitation, even if it is intercepted or compromised. However, encryption can also introduce overhead and complexity to edge computing environments, as it requires additional computational resources and may impact performance and latency. Therefore, organizations should carefully evaluate their encryption requirements and implement encryption selectively for sensitive data and communication channels where it is most needed. In summary, security challenges in edge environments require organizations to adopt a comprehensive and proactive approach to safeguarding sensitive data and protecting critical infrastructure from cyber threats. By addressing the unique security challenges of edge computing through a combination of lightweight security solutions, network segmentation, isolation, encryption, and access controls, organizations can strengthen the security posture of edge devices and ensure the confidentiality, integrity, and availability of data in edge environments.

Securing edge computing architectures is paramount for organizations aiming to protect sensitive data, ensure regulatory compliance, and maintain operational integrity in distributed computing environments. CLI commands such as netstat or nmap can be employed to conduct network scans and identify potential security *vulnerabilities or unauthorized network activity within edge computing architectures. One of the fundamental best practices for securing edge computing architectures is to implement robust authentication mechanisms, ensuring that only authorized users and devices can access critical resources and services. CLI commands such as ssh-keygen or openssl can be used to generate secure cryptographic keys and certificates for authentication purposes, enabling organizations to establish trust between edge devices and backend servers securely. By leveraging techniques such as multi-factor authentication (MFA) or biometric authentication, organizations can further strengthen access controls and protect against unauthorized access attempts or credential theft. Another critical best practice for securing edge computing architectures is to encrypt data both in transit and at rest to protect it from unauthorized access or interception. CLI commands such as gpg or openssl can be utilized to implement encryption algorithms and secure communication channels between edge devices and backend servers, ensuring the confidentiality and integrity of sensitive data transmitted over insecure networks. By encrypting data using strong cryptographic algorithms such as AES or RSA, organizations can prevent eavesdropping,* data tampering, and man-in-the-middle attacks, safeguarding sensitive information from unauthorized access or disclosure. Additionally, organizations should implement secure communication protocols such as HTTPS or TLS to encrypt data transmitted between edge devices and backend servers over untrusted networks, further enhancing data security and privacy. Network segmentation is another essential best practice for securing edge computing architectures, enabling organizations to divide their network into separate segments or zones based on security requirements and access controls. CLI commands such as iptables or firewalld can be used to configure network firewalls and access control lists (ACLs) to restrict traffic flow between different segments and prevent unauthorized access to critical resources or services. By isolating edge devices and applications from each other and from external networks, organizations can minimize the risk of lateral movement and limit the impact of security breaches or cyber attacks. Additionally, organizations should implement intrusion detection and prevention systems (IDS/IPS) to monitor network traffic and detect suspicious activity or anomalies indicative of security threats. CLI commands such as snort or suricata can be employed to deploy IDS/IPS sensors on edge devices or network gateways, enabling organizations to detect and mitigate security incidents in real-time. By analyzing network traffic patterns and identifying potential security threats, IDS/IPS systems can help organizations proactively defend against cyber attacks and prevent unauthorized access to sensitive data or resources. Regular security assessments and vulnerability scans are essential best practices for maintaining the security posture of edge computing architectures and identifying potential security weaknesses or gaps. CLI commands such as openvas or nessus can be used to conduct vulnerability scans and identify security vulnerabilities or misconfigurations within edge devices and network infrastructure, enabling organizations to prioritize and remediate security issues promptly. By performing regular security assessments and vulnerability scans, organizations can identify and mitigate security risks before they can be exploited by malicious actors, ensuring the integrity and resilience of their edge computing architectures. Furthermore, organizations should establish incident response and disaster recovery plans to respond to security incidents or breaches effectively. CLI commands such as tcpdump or wireshark can be utilized to capture and analyze network traffic during security incidents, enabling organizations to identify the root cause of the incident and implement corrective actions to mitigate its impact. By defining roles and responsibilities, establishing communication channels, and conducting regular training and drills, organizations can ensure an effective and coordinated response to security incidents, minimizing downtime and data loss in the event of a breach. In summary, implementing best practices for securing edge computing architectures is essential for organizations to protect sensitive data, maintain regulatory compliance, and mitigate the risk of cyber threats. By implementing robust authentication mechanisms, encrypting data, segmenting networks, deploying intrusion detection systems, conducting regular security assessments, and establishing incident response plans, organizations can strengthen the security posture of their edge computing architectures and ensure the integrity, confidentiality, and availability of their data and resources.

Chapter 9: Monitoring and Management Frameworks

Frameworks for monitoring edge infrastructure play a crucial role in ensuring the reliability, performance, and security of edge computing environments. CLI commands such as top or htop can be used to monitor system resource usage and performance metrics on edge devices, enabling organizations to identify and troubleshoot performance issues in real-time. One widely used framework for monitoring edge infrastructure is Prometheus, an open-source monitoring and alerting toolkit designed for monitoring cloud-native applications and microservices architectures. CLI commands such as wget or curl can be used to download and install Prometheus on edge devices, enabling organizations to collect and store time-series data metrics from various sources, including edge devices, applications, and network services. By deploying Prometheus agents on edge devices and configuring them to scrape metrics from target endpoints, organizations can monitor the health, performance, and availability of edge infrastructure components and detect anomalies or performance degradation *proactively. Another popular framework for monitoring edge infrastructure is Grafana, an open-source analytics and visualization platform that integrates seamlessly with Prometheus and other data sources to provide real-time insights and dashboards for monitoring and troubleshooting purposes. CLI commands such as docker or kubectl can be used to deploy Grafana alongside Prometheus on edge devices, enabling organizations to visualize and analyze performance metrics and telemetry data collected from edge infrastructure components. By creating custom dashboards and visualizations in Grafana, organizations can gain actionable insights into the operational status of edge devices, identify trends and patterns in performance metrics, and troubleshoot issues efficiently. Additionally, Grafana supports alerting and notification mechanisms, enabling organizations to define threshold-based alerts and receive notifications via email, Slack, or other channels when performance metrics exceed predefined thresholds or anomalies are detected. In addition to Prometheus and Grafana, organizations can leverage commercial monitoring solutions such as Datadog, New Relic, or Splunk to monitor edge infrastructure comprehensively. CLI commands such as apt or yum can be used to install and configure commercial monitoring agents on edge devices, enabling organizations to collect and analyze performance metrics, logs, and traces from distributed edge environments. By leveraging advanced analytics and machine learning capabilities, commercial monitoring solutions can provide organizations with deeper insights into the operational health and performance of edge infrastructure components, enabling them to identify and remediate issues proactively and optimize resource utilization and performance. Furthermore, commercial monitoring solutions typically offer integrations with other tools and platforms commonly used in edge computing environments, such as container orchestration systems, edge gateways, and IoT platforms, enabling organizations to centralize monitoring and management tasks and streamline operations. In summary, frameworks for monitoring edge infrastructure are essential for ensuring the reliability, performance, and security of edge computing environments. By leveraging open-source tools such as Prometheus and Grafana or commercial monitoring solutions, organizations can collect, analyze, and visualize performance metrics and telemetry data from edge devices, applications, and network services, enabling them to monitor the health and performance of edge infrastructure components, detect anomalies or performance degradation proactively, and optimize resource utilization and performance effectively. Management tools and techniques for edge environments are critical for efficiently deploying, configuring, and managing distributed computing resources and applications at the network edge. CLI commands such as Ansible or Terraform can be used to automate the provisioning and configuration of edge devices and infrastructure, enabling organizations to streamline deployment processes and ensure consistency across distributed environments. One popular management tool for edge environments is Kubernetes, an open-source container orchestration platform that enables organizations to automate the deployment, scaling, and management of containerized applications across clusters of edge devices. CLI commands such as kubectl can be used to deploy Kubernetes clusters on edge devices and manage containerized applications running on edge infrastructure, enabling organizations to abstract away the complexities of managing distributed computing resources and focus on developing and deploying applications. By leveraging Kubernetes, organizations can improve resource utilization, enhance scalability, and ensure high availability for edge applications, enabling them to deliver reliable and responsive services to end-users. Another management technique for edge environments is edge computing gateways, which act as intermediaries between edge devices and backend servers or cloud services, enabling organizations to aggregate, process, and analyze data locally before transmitting it to centralized data centers or cloud environments. CLI commands such as Docker or Kubernetes can be used to deploy edge computing gateways on edge devices, enabling organizations to implement edge intelligence and data processing capabilities at the network edge. By deploying edge computing gateways, organizations can reduce latency, bandwidth consumption, and reliance on centralized infrastructure, enabling them to deliver faster, more responsive services to end-users and optimize network traffic and resource usage. Additionally, edge computing gateways can provide local caching, pre-processing, and filtering capabilities, enabling organizations to reduce the volume of data transmitted over the network and improve the efficiency of data transmission and processing in edge environments. Another management technique for edge environments is edge-native application development, which involves designing and developing applications specifically for deployment and execution at the network edge. CLI commands such as Git or SVN can be used to version control application code and manage collaboration among developers, enabling organizations to track changes and maintain code quality throughout the development lifecycle. By leveraging edge-native application development, organizations can optimize performance, reduce latency, and improve reliability for edge applications, enabling them to deliver fast, responsive services to end-users and support emerging use cases such as IoT, augmented reality, and real-time analytics. Additionally, edge-native applications can leverage edge-specific APIs and libraries to access local resources and services, enabling organizations to maximize the capabilities of edge devices and infrastructure and deliver differentiated services to end-users. Another management technique for edge environments is edge monitoring and analytics, which involves collecting, analyzing, and visualizing telemetry data and performance metrics from edge devices and infrastructure to monitor operational health, detect anomalies, and optimize resource usage. CLI commands such as Prometheus or Grafana can be used to deploy monitoring and analytics tools* on edge devices, enabling organizations to collect and analyze performance metrics and telemetry data in real-time. By leveraging edge monitoring and analytics, organizations can gain actionable insights into the operational status of edge infrastructure components, identify trends and patterns in performance metrics, and troubleshoot issues proactively. Additionally, edge monitoring and analytics can support predictive maintenance, anomaly detection, and performance optimization use cases, enabling organizations to improve the reliability, efficiency, and resilience of edge environments. In summary, management tools and techniques for edge environments are essential for efficiently deploying, configuring, and managing distributed computing resources and applications at the network edge. By leveraging automation, container orchestration, edge computing gateways, edge-native application development, and edge monitoring and analytics, organizations can optimize resource utilization, improve performance, and enhance reliability for edge applications, enabling them to deliver fast, responsive services to end-users and support emerging use cases in IoT, augmented reality, and real-time analytics.

Chapter 10: Case Studies: Successful Architectural Implementations

Real-world examples of effective edge computing architectures abound in various industries, showcasing the versatility and impact of edge technologies in transforming business operations and customer experiences. In the retail sector, companies like Walmart have embraced edge computing to enhance inventory management, optimize supply chain logistics, and deliver personalized customer experiences in brick-and-mortar stores. By deploying edge devices such as smart shelves and inventory trackers, retailers can monitor product availability in real-time, analyze customer purchasing patterns, and automate inventory replenishment processes, ensuring shelves are stocked with the right products at the right time. CLI commands such as docker or kubectl can be used to deploy edge applications and services on IoT devices and edge servers, enabling retailers to implement edge intelligence and data processing capabilities at the point of sale. Additionally, edge computing enables retailers to deliver personalized shopping experiences by leveraging real-time customer data and location-based services to offer targeted promotions, discounts, and recommendations to shoppers based on their preferences and purchasing history. In the healthcare industry, edge computing is revolutionizing patient care delivery, enabling healthcare providers to deliver remote monitoring, telemedicine, and predictive analytics services to patients anytime, anywhere. Companies like Philips have developed edge-enabled healthcare solutions that leverage IoT devices, wearables, and medical sensors to monitor patient vital signs, collect health data, and provide real-time insights to healthcare professionals. CLI commands such as ssh or scp can be used to securely access and transfer patient data and medical records between edge devices and backend servers, ensuring data privacy and compliance with regulatory requirements such as HIPAA. By deploying edge computing solutions, healthcare providers can improve patient outcomes, reduce hospital readmissions, and lower healthcare costs by enabling early detection and intervention for chronic conditions, optimizing treatment plans, and enhancing patient engagement and adherence to care plans. In the manufacturing sector, edge computing is transforming industrial operations by enabling real-time monitoring, predictive maintenance, and *process optimization across the factory floor. Companies like Siemens have developed edge-enabled manufacturing solutions that leverage IoT sensors, industrial robots, and edge computing technologies to monitor equipment health, detect anomalies, and optimize production workflows in real-time. CLI commands such as Ansible or Terraform can be used to automate the deployment and configuration of edge devices and industrial sensors, enabling manufacturers to scale their edge computing infrastructure and monitor and manage distributed manufacturing processes efficiently. By deploying edge computing solutions, manufacturers can improve operational efficiency, reduce downtime, and increase product quality by enabling predictive maintenance, optimizing equipment performance, and minimizing production bottlenecks. In the transportation sector, edge computing is revolutionizing logistics and fleet management by enabling real-time tracking, monitoring, and optimization of vehicles and cargo. Companies like FedEx have deployed edge-enabled logistics solutions that leverage GPS trackers, telematics devices, and edge computing technologies to monitor vehicle location, route efficiency, and cargo condition in real-time. CLI commands such as wget or curl can be used to download and install edge computing software on* vehicles and logistics hubs, enabling transportation companies to collect and analyze telemetry data and performance metrics from edge devices and optimize fleet operations. By leveraging edge computing solutions, transportation companies can improve delivery accuracy, reduce fuel consumption, and minimize transportation costs by optimizing route planning, vehicle utilization, and cargo handling processes in real-time. In summary, real-world examples of effective edge computing architectures demonstrate the transformative potential of edge technologies in various industries, from retail and healthcare to manufacturing and transportation. By leveraging edge computing solutions, organizations can unlock new opportunities for innovation, improve operational efficiency, and deliver personalized experiences to customers, enabling them to stay ahead of the competition and thrive in the digital era.

Lessons learned from successful case studies in the realm of edge computing provide invaluable insights into the practical applications, challenges, and best practices associated with deploying and managing edge environments. CLI commands such as docker or kubectl can be used to deploy edge computing solutions, enabling organizations to implement edge intelligence and data processing capabilities at the network edge. One of the key lessons gleaned from successful case studies is the importance of aligning edge computing initiatives with organizational goals and business objectives. By defining clear use cases and success criteria upfront, organizations can ensure that edge computing projects deliver tangible value and address specific pain points or business challenges. Additionally, successful case studies underscore the significance of selecting the right hardware and software infrastructure for edge deployments. CLI commands such as apt or yum can be used to install and configure edge computing software on edge devices, enabling organizations to collect, process, and analyze data locally before transmitting it to centralized data centers or cloud environments. By leveraging edge-native applications and lightweight containers, organizations can optimize resource usage, reduce latency, and improve reliability for edge applications, enabling them to deliver fast, responsive services to end-users. Furthermore, successful case studies highlight the importance of robust security measures and compliance practices in edge computing deployments. CLI commands such as ssh-keygen or openssl can be used to generate secure cryptographic keys and *certificates for authentication purposes, enabling organizations to establish trust between edge devices and backend servers securely. By encrypting data both in transit and at rest, organizations can protect sensitive information from unauthorized access or interception and ensure compliance with regulatory requirements such as GDPR or CCPA. Moreover, successful case studies emphasize the need for continuous monitoring, performance optimization, and scalability planning in edge computing environments. CLI commands such as Prometheus or Grafana can be used to deploy monitoring and analytics tools on edge devices, enabling organizations to collect and analyze performance metrics and telemetry data in real-time. By leveraging predictive analytics and machine learning algorithms, organizations can proactively identify and mitigate performance bottlenecks, predict equipment failures, and optimize resource allocation in edge environments. Additionally, successful case studies underscore the importance of collaboration and partnerships in driving innovation and accelerating edge computing adoption. By collaborating with technology vendors, industry partners, and academic institutions, organizations can leverage expertise, share best practices, and co-create solutions* tailored to specific industry verticals and use cases. Furthermore, successful case studies highlight the significance of user-centric design and iterative development methodologies in edge computing projects. By soliciting feedback from end-users and stakeholders early and often, organizations can identify usability issues, validate assumptions, and iterate on solutions to ensure they meet user needs and expectations. In summary, lessons learned from successful case studies in edge computing underscore the importance of strategic alignment, infrastructure selection, security and compliance, monitoring and optimization, collaboration and partnerships, and user-centric design in driving successful edge computing deployments. By adopting a holistic approach and incorporating these lessons into their edge computing strategies, organizations can unlock new opportunities for innovation, efficiency, and competitive advantage in the digital age.

BOOK 3
ADVANCED EDGE COMPUTING
SCALABILITY, SECURITY, AND OPTIMIZATION
STRATEGIES

ROB BOTWRIGHT

Chapter 1: Scaling Edge Computing Infrastructure

Horizontal and vertical scaling are two fundamental strategies for increasing the capacity and performance of computing systems, each with its own set of considerations and trade-offs. CLI commands such as Docker or Kubernetes can be used to horizontally scale applications by deploying multiple instances across a cluster of servers or virtual machines, enabling organizations to distribute workloads evenly and handle increased traffic or demand more effectively. In horizontal scaling, also known as scaling out, additional resources are added to the system by provisioning more instances of the application, allowing organizations to accommodate growing user bases, handle spikes in traffic, and improve fault tolerance and availability. However, horizontal scaling may require changes to the application architecture and infrastructure to support distributed computing and data replication, and it may introduce complexity in managing and orchestrating multiple instances across a cluster. On the other hand, vertical scaling, also known as scaling up, involves adding more resources, such as CPU, memory, or storage, to existing instances of the application, enabling organizations to increase capacity and performance without changing the underlying architecture. CLI commands such as SSH or SCP can be used to connect to virtual machines or cloud instances and upgrade hardware specifications or allocate additional resources, such as CPU cores or RAM, to meet growing demand or workload requirements. Vertical scaling offers simplicity and ease of management, as organizations can scale resources vertically without modifying application code or infrastructure configurations, and it may be more cost-effective for workloads with predictable or steady growth patterns.

However, vertical scaling has limitations in terms of scalability and resource availability, as it may reach hardware or software constraints, such as CPU limits or memory saturation, and it may result in single points of failure and decreased fault tolerance and availability. When deciding between horizontal and vertical scaling strategies, organizations should consider factors such as scalability requirements, workload characteristics, performance objectives, cost considerations, and operational complexity. CLI commands such as Ansible or Terraform can be used to automate the provisioning and management of infrastructure resources, enabling organizations to scale applications horizontally or vertically based on workload demands and business needs. Additionally, organizations can leverage cloud computing services and platforms, such as Amazon Web Services (AWS) or Microsoft Azure, to dynamically scale resources up or down in response to changing traffic patterns or demand spikes, using CLI commands such as AWS CLI or Azure CLI to programmatically manage and scale cloud resources. By combining horizontal and vertical scaling strategies with automation and cloud-native technologies, organizations can build scalable, resilient, and cost-effective computing systems that meet the demands of modern applications and workloads in a dynamic and evolving digital landscape.

Dynamic resource allocation in edge environments is a critical aspect of optimizing performance, scalability, and resource utilization in distributed computing systems deployed at the network edge. CLI commands such as Docker or Kubernetes can be used to dynamically allocate resources, such as CPU, memory, or storage, to edge devices or applications based on workload demands and availability, enabling organizations to adapt to *changing conditions and ensure efficient resource utilization. The dynamic nature of edge environments, characterized by fluctuating workloads, varying network conditions, and resource constraints, necessitates flexible and adaptive resource management strategies to meet service-level objectives and deliver optimal user experiences. By leveraging containerization and orchestration technologies, organizations can achieve dynamic resource allocation by defining resource requests and limits for containerized applications and leveraging auto-scaling mechanisms to adjust resource allocations dynamically based on workload demands and resource availability.*

CLI commands such as kubectl can be used to configure Kubernetes auto-scaling policies, enabling organizations to scale up or down the number of application instances based on metrics such as CPU utilization, memory usage, or request latency, ensuring that applications have the resources they need to handle peak loads and maintain responsiveness. Additionally, organizations can implement dynamic resource allocation policies based on edge computing paradigms such as fog computing or mobile edge computing, which involve distributing computing resources and services closer to end-users or devices at the network edge. CLI commands such as Ansible or Terraform can be used to automate the deployment and management of edge computing infrastructure, enabling organizations to provision, configure, and scale edge resources dynamically based on factors such as location, proximity to end-users, and network conditions. By deploying edge computing gateways or edge servers in proximity to edge devices or sensors, organizations can minimize latency, reduce bandwidth consumption, and improve data locality, enabling them to deliver faster, more responsive services and support emerging use cases such as IoT, augmented reality, and real-time analytics. Furthermore, organizations can leverage edge-native application development frameworks and tools to optimize resource usage and performance for edge applications, enabling them to maximize the efficiency and effectiveness of resource allocation in edge environments.

CLI commands such as Git or SVN can be used to version control application code and manage collaboration among developers, enabling organizations to track changes, maintain code quality, and deploy updates to edge applications seamlessly. By adopting a holistic approach to *dynamic resource allocation in edge environments, organizations can optimize performance, scalability, and resource utilization, enabling them to deliver reliable, responsive services to end-users and support emerging use cases and applications in a rapidly evolving digital landscape.*

Chapter 2: Advanced Networking Techniques for Scalability

Software-defined networking (SDN) plays a pivotal role in the evolution of edge computing, offering dynamic and programmable network management capabilities that are essential for efficiently orchestrating distributed computing resources and services at the network edge. CLI commands such as OpenFlow or Mininet can be used to deploy SDN controllers and switches, enabling organizations to centralize network control and automate the configuration and management of edge networking infrastructure. The traditional networking paradigm, characterized by static and hardware-centric network configurations, is ill-suited for the dynamic and heterogeneous nature of edge environments, where devices, applications, and services are distributed across geographically dispersed locations with varying connectivity requirements and resource constraints. SDN enables organizations to abstract network control and management functions from underlying hardware and implement policies and configurations dynamically through software-

based controllers, enabling them to adapt to changing conditions and requirements in edge environments. By decoupling the control plane from the data plane, SDN enables organizations to centralize network intelligence and programmatically configure and manage network resources based on application requirements and business policies, rather than relying on manual configuration and provisioning processes. CLI commands such as OVS or Ryu can be used to configure Open vSwitch (OVS) instances and Ryu controllers, enabling organizations to build and manage SDN-based networks in edge environments. SDN also facilitates network virtualization and abstraction, enabling organizations to create logical network overlays and segments that span across multiple physical and virtual infrastructure components, providing isolation, scalability, and flexibility for edge applications and services. By leveraging SDN technologies such as virtual switches, tunnels, and overlays, organizations can create virtualized network environments that are decoupled from underlying physical infrastructure, enabling them to deploy and manage edge applications and services more efficiently. SDN enables organizations to implement network policies and configurations dynamically, allowing them to enforce security, quality of service (QoS), and traffic management rules consistently across distributed edge environments. CLI commands such as iptables or tc can be used to configure firewall rules, traffic shaping, and quality of service (QoS) policies in SDN-based networks, enabling organizations to control and prioritize network traffic based on application requirements and business priorities. SDN also facilitates network automation and orchestration, enabling organizations to streamline network provisioning, configuration, and management processes through programmable interfaces and APIs. By integrating SDN controllers with orchestration frameworks such as Kubernetes or OpenStack, organizations can automate the deployment and management of edge applications and services, enabling them to scale and adapt to changing demand and conditions in real-time. SDN enables organizations to implement network slicing and service chaining, enabling them to partition and customize network resources and services for different edge applications and use cases. CLI commands such as NSH or SFC can be used to configure service function chaining (SFC) and network slicing policies in SDN-based networks, enabling organizations to create customized network service chains and segments tailored to specific application requirements and traffic flows. SDN facilitates network monitoring and analytics, enabling organizations to collect, analyze, and visualize network performance metrics and telemetry data in real-time. By integrating SDN controllers with monitoring and analytics platforms such as Grafana or Prometheus, organizations can gain visibility into network behavior, identify performance bottlenecks, and troubleshoot issues proactively, enabling them to optimize network performance and reliability in edge environments. In summary, SDN is a foundational technology for edge computing, offering dynamic and programmable network management capabilities that are essential for efficiently orchestrating distributed computing resources and services at the network edge. By decoupling network control from underlying hardware and implementing policies and configurations through software-based controllers, SDN enables organizations to adapt to changing conditions and requirements in edge environments, streamline network provisioning and management processes, and deliver reliable, responsive services to end-users.

Network Function Virtualization (NFV) stands as a transformative technology in the realm of edge computing, offering organizations a scalable and flexible approach to deploying network services and functions at the network edge. CLI commands such as Ansible or Terraform can be utilized to automate the deployment and management of virtualized network functions (VNFs) in edge environments, streamlining operations and ensuring consistency across distributed infrastructure. In traditional networking architectures, network services and functions are typically implemented using specialized hardware appliances, leading to inflexibility, high costs, and complexity in managing and scaling network infrastructure. NFV addresses these challenges by decoupling network functions from proprietary hardware and implementing them as software-based instances that can be deployed and managed dynamically on commodity hardware or virtualized environments. CLI commands such as docker or docker-compose can be leveraged to deploy and manage containerized network functions (CNFs) in edge environments, enabling organizations to achieve greater agility, scalability, and cost efficiency in delivering network services. By virtualizing network functions such as firewalls, load balancers, routers, and intrusion detection systems, NFV enables organizations to consolidate and abstract network *services, reducing hardware dependencies and enabling more flexible and efficient resource allocation. NFV also facilitates service chaining and orchestration, enabling organizations to compose and automate complex network service workflows dynamically, based on application requirements and business policies. CLI commands such as Kubernetes or Helm can be employed to orchestrate the deployment and scaling of network services and functions in edge environments, ensuring seamless integration and interoperability across distributed infrastructure components. Moreover, NFV enables organizations to implement network services and functions closer to end-users and devices at the network edge, reducing latency, improving performance, and enhancing user experiences for latency-sensitive applications such as IoT, real-time analytics, and content delivery. By deploying VNFs and CNFs at the network edge, organizations can minimize traffic backhaul to centralized data centers or cloud environments, reducing bandwidth consumption and optimizing network resource utilization. NFV also enables organizations to achieve greater resilience and fault tolerance in edge environments, by dynamically scaling network functions in response to changing demand and conditions, and by leveraging automated failover and redundancy mechanisms to ensure high availability and reliability. CLI commands such as curl or wget can be used to download and install NFV management and orchestration (MANO) frameworks, enabling organizations to automate the lifecycle management of virtualized network functions and services in edge environments. Additionally, NFV facilitates network slicing and multi-tenancy, enabling organizations to create isolated and customized network segments for different users, applications, or services, while ensuring resource isolation, security, and performance guarantees. By leveraging NFV technologies and principles, organizations can accelerate innovation, reduce costs, and enhance agility in deploying and managing network services and functions in edge environments, enabling them to deliver scalable, resilient, and cost-effective networking solutions that meet the demands of modern applications and workloads in a dynamic and evolving digital landscape.*

Chapter 3: Data Processing Optimization at the Edge

In-memory computing techniques represent a groundbreaking approach to edge data processing, revolutionizing how organizations leverage data for real-time insights and decision-making at the network edge. CLI commands such as Redis or Memcached can be employed to deploy and manage in-memory data stores in edge environments, providing high-performance data processing capabilities that enable organizations to analyze, transform, and act upon data with unprecedented speed and efficiency. Traditional data processing architectures often rely on disk-based storage systems, which can introduce latency and bottlenecks in data access and retrieval, especially in distributed edge environments where data must travel across network boundaries to centralized data centers or cloud platforms. In contrast, in-memory computing techniques leverage volatile memory, such as RAM, to store and process data directly in-memory, eliminating the need for disk I/O operations and significantly reducing latency and overhead associated with data processing. By storing data in-memory, organizations can achieve faster read and write speeds, enabling real-time data ingestion, analysis, and response for latency-sensitive applications such as IoT, machine learning, and predictive analytics. CLI commands such as Apache Ignite or Apache Geode can be utilized to deploy distributed in-memory computing platforms in edge environments, enabling organizations to scale out data processing capabilities horizontally across multiple edge devices or nodes, while maintaining low-latency access to data and ensuring high availability and fault tolerance. In-memory computing techniques also enable organizations to implement complex data processing pipelines and workflows at the network edge, leveraging parallel processing and distributed computing paradigms to analyze and transform large volumes of data in real-time. By distributing data processing tasks across multiple nodes or devices, organizations can achieve greater throughput and scalability, enabling them to handle growing data volumes and support emerging use cases such as edge AI, video analytics, and autonomous systems. CLI commands such as Apache Kafka or Apache Flink can be employed to deploy stream processing frameworks in edge environments, enabling organizations to ingest, process, and analyze data streams in real-time, while maintaining low-latency and high-throughput processing capabilities. In-memory computing techniques also facilitate the implementation of event-driven architectures and microservices architectures at the network edge, enabling organizations to build scalable and responsive applications that react to events and changes in real-time. By leveraging in-memory data stores and caching mechanisms, organizations can cache frequently accessed data and computations in-memory, reducing the need for repeated disk I/O operations and improving overall application performance and responsiveness. CLI commands such as Apache Kafka Streams or Apache Pulsar can be used to deploy event-driven architectures and messaging systems in edge environments, enabling organizations to build event-driven applications that process and react to events in real-time, while ensuring low-latency and high-throughput data processing capabilities. In summary, in-memory computing techniques represent a transformative approach to edge data processing, enabling organizations to unlock the full potential of their data for real-time insights and decision-making at the network edge. By leveraging in-memory data stores, distributed computing platforms, and stream processing frameworks, organizations can *achieve faster data processing speeds, lower latency, and greater scalability, enabling them to deliver innovative and responsive applications and services that meet the demands of today's digital economy.*

Chapter 4: Security Challenges in Advanced Edge Environments

The emerging threat landscape in advanced edge environments presents a complex and evolving challenge for organizations deploying distributed computing resources and services at the network edge. CLI commands such as nmap or Metasploit can be utilized to conduct vulnerability assessments and penetration tests in edge environments, enabling organizations to identify and mitigate potential security risks and vulnerabilities before they are exploited by malicious actors. As edge computing continues to gain traction and adoption across various industries, it brings with it a new set of security concerns and attack vectors that organizations must address to safeguard their data, applications, and infrastructure from cyber threats. The distributed nature of edge environments, characterized by a multitude of interconnected devices, sensors, and systems deployed at the network edge, introduces new points of entry and potential vulnerabilities that attackers can exploit to gain unauthorized access or disrupt operations. CLI commands such as *iptables or pfSense can be employed to configure firewall rules and access control policies in edge environments, enabling organizations to control inbound and outbound network traffic and protect against unauthorized access and malicious activities. One of the key challenges in securing advanced edge environments is the sheer scale and diversity of devices and endpoints connected to the network, ranging from IoT devices and sensors to edge servers and gateways, each with its own unique security requirements and vulnerabilities. CLI commands such as Nessus or OpenVAS can be used to scan and assess the security posture of devices and endpoints in edge environments, enabling organizations to identify vulnerabilities, misconfigurations, and potential security weaknesses that could be exploited by attackers. In addition to device-level vulnerabilities, edge environments are also susceptible to attacks targeting the network infrastructure and communication protocols that facilitate data exchange and connectivity between edge devices and systems. CLI commands such as Wireshark or tcpdump can be employed to monitor network traffic and analyze communication patterns in edge environments, enabling organizations to detect and mitigate anomalous activities, such as unauthorized access attempts, data exfiltration, or denial-of-service (DoS) attacks. Another emerging threat in advanced edge environments is the proliferation of malware and ransomware targeting edge devices and systems, seeking to exploit vulnerabilities and compromise data integrity, availability, and confidentiality. CLI commands such as ClamAV or Sophos can be used to deploy endpoint protection solutions in edge environments, enabling organizations to detect and quarantine malicious software and prevent malware infections from spreading across the network. Moreover, the dynamic and ephemeral nature of edge computing workloads introduces new challenges for security operations teams, who must continuously monitor, analyze, and respond to security incidents and threats in real-time. CLI commands such as Suricata or Snort can be employed to deploy intrusion detection and prevention systems (IDPS) in edge environments, enabling organizations to detect and block suspicious network traffic and activities, such as port scanning, brute force attacks, or SQL injection attempts. As organizations continue to adopt edge computing technologies to support mission-critical applications and services, it is imperative that they implement comprehensive security measures and best practices to mitigate the risks and challenges associated with the emerging threat landscape in advanced edge environments. CLI commands such as SELinux or AppArmor can be used to implement mandatory access controls and application sandboxing in edge environments, enabling organizations to limit the privileges and permissions of applications and services and prevent them from accessing or modifying sensitive data or system resources. By taking a proactive and holistic approach to security, organizations can build resilient and secure edge environments that enable them to leverage the benefits of edge computing while protecting against emerging cyber threats and attacks. Zero Trust security models have emerged as a critical paradigm shift in cybersecurity, especially in the context of advanced edge architectures where traditional perimeter-based security approaches are no longer sufficient to protect against sophisticated threats and attacks. CLI commands such as ssh-keygen or openssl can be used to generate cryptographic keys and certificates for implementing authentication and encryption mechanisms in zero trust security architectures, ensuring secure communication and access control between edge devices and services. The Zero Trust approach challenges the conventional notion of trust by assuming that threats may already exist within the network and therefore, every user, device, and transaction must be authenticated, authorized, and encrypted, regardless of their location or proximity to the network perimeter. CLI commands such as iptables or pfSense can be employed to configure micro-segmentation and network segmentation policies in zero trust security architectures, enabling organizations to enforce granular access controls and isolate sensitive data and workloads from unauthorized access or lateral movement by attackers. By adopting a Zero Trust security model, organizations can enhance their security posture and resilience by minimizing the attack surface, reducing the risk of insider threats and lateral movement, and ensuring continuous monitoring and enforcement of security policies across distributed edge environments. CLI commands such as OpenVPN or WireGuard can be used to deploy secure VPN tunnels and encrypted communication channels in zero trust security architectures, enabling organizations to establish secure connectivity and access control between remote users, devices, and edge resources without exposing sensitive data or services to potential threats. Zero Trust security architectures rely on a combination of identity and access management (IAM), encryption, network segmentation, and* continuous monitoring and analytics to verify and validate the identity, trustworthiness, and integrity of users, devices, and applications before granting access to resources or data. CLI commands such as LDAP or Active Directory can be employed to implement centralized identity and access management systems in zero trust security architectures, enabling organizations to authenticate and authorize users and devices based on their roles, permissions, and trust levels, and enforce consistent access controls across distributed edge environments. The principle of least privilege is a core tenet of Zero Trust security models, which advocates for granting users and devices only the minimum level of access required to perform their intended tasks or functions, and revoking access privileges as soon as they are no longer needed. CLI commands such as sudo or su can be used to implement privilege escalation and de-escalation mechanisms in zero trust security architectures, enabling organizations to restrict administrative privileges and minimize the risk of privilege abuse or credential theft by attackers. In addition to access controls and authentication mechanisms, encryption plays a crucial role in Zero Trust security architectures, ensuring the confidentiality and integrity of data in transit and at rest, and protecting against eavesdropping, tampering, and data breaches. CLI commands such as GPG or OpenSSL can be employed to encrypt data and communications in zero trust security architectures, enabling organizations to secure sensitive information and prevent unauthorized access or disclosure. Continuous monitoring and analytics are essential components of Zero Trust security architectures, enabling organizations to detect and respond to security threats and anomalies in real-time, and adapt their security posture dynamically to mitigate risks and vulnerabilities. CLI commands such as tcpdump or Wireshark can be used to capture and analyze network traffic in zero trust security architectures, enabling organizations to identify suspicious activities, unauthorized access attempts, or anomalous behavior, and take appropriate remediation actions to mitigate potential security risks and incidents. In summary, Zero Trust security models offer a proactive and adaptive approach to cybersecurity, enabling organizations to establish a robust security perimeter around their distributed edge environments, and protect against emerging threats and attacks. By implementing comprehensive access controls, authentication mechanisms, encryption protocols, and continuous monitoring and analytics, organizations can build *resilient and secure edge architectures that enable them to leverage the benefits of edge computing while safeguarding their data, applications, and infrastructure against potential security risks and vulnerabilities.*

Chapter 5: Encryption and Authentication Strategies

Advanced Encryption Standards (AES) stand as a cornerstone of modern cryptographic techniques, providing robust security mechanisms to safeguard data confidentiality and integrity in edge computing environments. CLI commands such as OpenSSL or GnuPG can be utilized to generate AES keys and implement encryption and decryption operations in edge security architectures, ensuring that sensitive data remains protected from unauthorized access or tampering. AES, adopted by the National Institute of Standards and Technology (NIST) in 2001, represents a symmetric key encryption algorithm capable of securing data at rest and in transit across various computing platforms and communication channels. With its flexibility and efficiency, AES has become a widely adopted standard for securing data in edge computing scenarios where resource-constrained devices and low-latency requirements demand lightweight yet robust encryption solutions. CLI commands such as ssh-keygen or OpenSSL can be employed to generate AES keys with varying key sizes (e.g.,

128-bit, 192-bit, or 256-bit), enabling organizations to tailor their encryption mechanisms to meet specific security requirements and performance constraints in edge environments. The strength of AES lies in its ability to transform plaintext data into ciphertext using a symmetric key, which can then be securely transmitted or stored without fear of interception or unauthorized access. CLI commands such as bcrypt or scrypt can be utilized to implement key derivation functions (KDFs) in edge security architectures, enabling organizations to derive AES keys from user passwords or other secret values, enhancing the security of cryptographic operations and protecting against brute force attacks. While AES encryption provides robust protection against eavesdropping and data interception, it is essential to complement encryption with secure key management practices to prevent unauthorized access to encryption keys and ensure the long-term security of encrypted data. CLI commands such as OpenSSL or GnuPG can be employed to implement key management protocols and mechanisms in edge security architectures, enabling organizations to securely generate, store, distribute, and rotate AES keys as needed to maintain data confidentiality and integrity over time. AES encryption can be applied to various data types and communication channels in edge environments, including sensor data, telemetry streams, command and control messages, and inter-device communications, ensuring end-to-end security and privacy across the edge ecosystem. CLI commands such as OpenSSL or GnuPG can be used to encrypt and decrypt data using AES in edge security architectures, enabling organizations to protect sensitive information and prevent unauthorized access or tampering by malicious actors. With its widespread adoption and proven security properties, AES encryption serves as a foundational building block for implementing secure edge computing solutions that meet the stringent security requirements of modern applications and workloads. CLI commands such as OpenSSL or GnuPG can be employed to integrate AES encryption into existing edge computing platforms and frameworks, enabling organizations to enhance the security posture of their edge deployments and protect sensitive data against potential threats and vulnerabilities. In summary, AES encryption plays a vital role in ensuring data security and privacy in edge computing environments, enabling organizations to leverage the benefits of edge computing while safeguarding their data assets against *unauthorized access, interception, and tampering. Multi-Factor Authentication (MFA) represents a cornerstone of modern cybersecurity practices, providing an additional layer of protection to secure user accounts and access to sensitive resources in edge environments. CLI commands such as Google Authenticator or Authy can be employed to deploy MFA solutions in edge environments, enabling organizations to enhance the security of their authentication mechanisms and protect against unauthorized access or account compromise. MFA strengthens authentication by requiring users to provide multiple forms of verification, typically combining something they know (e.g., a password or PIN) with something they have (e.g., a smartphone or hardware token) or something they are (e.g., biometric data such as fingerprints or facial recognition). CLI commands such as pam_google_authenticator or pam_yubico can be used to integrate MFA with existing authentication systems in edge environments, enabling organizations to enforce strong authentication policies and mitigate the risk of credential theft or brute force attacks. By requiring users to provide multiple factors of authentication, MFA significantly reduces the likelihood of unauthorized access to sensitive* systems and data, even if one factor (such as a password) is compromised or stolen. CLI commands such as ssh-keygen or pam_radius can be employed to configure MFA for remote access to edge devices and systems, enabling organizations to enforce strong authentication controls and protect against unauthorized access from remote or external networks. MFA can be implemented using a variety of authentication factors, including one-time passwords (OTPs) generated by mobile apps or hardware tokens, biometric authentication methods such as fingerprint or facial recognition, or out-of-band verification mechanisms such as SMS or email. CLI commands such as pam_oath or pam_fprintd can be utilized to integrate OTP-based MFA solutions with authentication systems in edge environments, enabling organizations to add an additional layer of security to their login processes and prevent unauthorized access to sensitive resources. Biometric authentication methods, such as fingerprint or facial recognition, offer a convenient and secure way to verify users' identities in edge environments, leveraging unique physiological traits to authenticate users and grant access to systems and data. CLI commands such as pam_bioapi or pam_facialrecognition can be employed to deploy biometric authentication *solutions in edge environments, enabling organizations to enhance the security of their authentication mechanisms and provide a seamless user experience for accessing resources. Out-of-band verification mechanisms, such as SMS or email, offer an additional layer of security by requiring users to confirm their identity through a separate communication channel before granting access to sensitive resources. CLI commands such as pam_exec or pam_script can be used to implement out-of-band verification mechanisms in edge environments, enabling organizations to enforce strong authentication controls and protect against account takeover attacks. While MFA enhances security by requiring multiple factors of authentication, it is essential for organizations to balance security with usability and convenience to ensure a positive user experience. CLI commands such as pam_unix or pam_winbind can be employed to configure MFA policies and authentication methods in edge environments, enabling organizations to strike the right balance between security and usability and protect against unauthorized access to sensitive resources. In summary, MFA plays a crucial role in securing access to sensitive resources in edge environments, providing an additional layer of protection against unauthorized access and account compromise. By implementing MFA solutions that leverage multiple factors of authentication, organizations can enhance the security of their edge deployments and protect against a wide range of cybersecurity threats and attacks.*

Chapter 6: Threat Detection and Intrusion Prevention

Intrusion Detection Systems (IDS) represent a critical component of edge security architectures, providing real-time monitoring and detection of suspicious activities and security threats in distributed computing environments. CLI commands such as Snort or Suricata can be deployed to implement IDS solutions in edge environments, enabling organizations to detect and respond to potential security incidents and attacks before they can cause harm or damage. IDS systems work by analyzing network traffic, system logs, and other data sources to identify patterns and anomalies indicative of unauthorized access attempts, malicious activities, or policy violations.

CLI commands such as tcpdump or Wireshark can be utilized to capture and analyze network traffic in edge environments, providing valuable insights into potential security threats and vulnerabilities that may require further investigation or mitigation. There are two primary types of IDS: network-based IDS (NIDS) and host-based IDS

(HIDS), each serving a distinct role in monitoring and protecting edge environments against cybersecurity threats. CLI commands such as Snort or Suricata can be deployed as NIDS solutions in edge environments, enabling organizations to monitor network traffic for signs of suspicious behavior, such as port scanning, denial-of-service (DoS) attacks, or exploitation attempts targeting known vulnerabilities. On the other hand, CLI commands such as OSSEC or Tripwire can be deployed as HIDS solutions in edge environments, enabling organizations to monitor system logs, file integrity, and other host-level activities for signs of unauthorized access, malware infections, or system compromise. IDS solutions can be deployed in various deployment modes, including inline, passive, and hybrid modes, depending on the specific security requirements and operational constraints of the edge environment.

CLI commands such as iptables or Snort-inline can be used to configure inline IDS deployments in edge environments, enabling organizations to intercept and block malicious traffic in real-time before it reaches its intended target. Passive IDS deployments, on the other hand, monitor network traffic passively without interfering with the flow of data, enabling organizations to detect and analyze security threats without disrupting network operations or introducing additional latency. CLI commands such as Suricata or Zeek can be deployed as passive IDS solutions in edge environments, enabling organizations to monitor network traffic for signs of suspicious behavior and alert security personnel to potential security incidents. Hybrid IDS deployments combine elements of both inline and passive detection modes, enabling organizations to benefit from real-time threat prevention capabilities while also maintaining visibility into network traffic for analysis and forensic purposes. CLI commands such as Snort or Suricata can be configured to operate in hybrid mode in edge environments, enabling organizations to strike the right balance between security and performance based on their specific security requirements and operational constraints. IDS solutions generate alerts and notifications when suspicious activities or security threats are detected, enabling security personnel to investigate and respond to potential security incidents in a timely manner. CLI commands such as Snort or Suricata can be configured to send alerts to a centralized Security Information and Event Management (SIEM) system for further analysis and correlation with other security events and logs from across the organization. In addition to generating alerts, IDS solutions can also take automated response actions, such as blocking or quarantining suspicious traffic, updating firewall rules, or triggering incident response workflows, to mitigate potential security risks and prevent further damage or compromise. CLI commands such as iptables or Snort-inline can be configured to take automated response actions in edge environments, enabling organizations to respond to security threats in real-time and minimize the impact of potential security incidents on their operations and data. In summary, IDS solutions play a crucial role in enhancing the security posture of edge environments, enabling organizations to detect and respond to potential security threats and attacks in real-time, protect sensitive data and resources, and maintain the integrity and availability of their edge deployments. By deploying IDS solutions that leverage advanced detection techniques and automation capabilities, organizations can strengthen their defense-in-depth strategies and safeguard their edge environments against a wide range of cybersecurity threats and vulnerabilities.

Machine learning-based threat detection represents a cutting-edge approach to enhancing cybersecurity defenses at the edge, leveraging advanced algorithms and models to detect and mitigate security threats in real-time. CLI commands such as TensorFlow or Scikit-learn can be deployed to implement machine learning-based threat detection solutions in edge environments, enabling organizations to analyze vast amounts of data and identify patterns indicative of malicious activities or anomalous behavior. Machine learning algorithms can be trained on historical data collected from edge devices and systems to recognize normal patterns of behavior and identify deviations that may indicate a potential security threat or intrusion attempt.

CLI commands such as pandas or NumPy can be used to preprocess and analyze data sets in preparation for training machine learning models in edge environments, enabling organizations to extract valuable insights and features from raw data to improve the accuracy and effectiveness of threat detection algorithms. Supervised learning techniques, such as classification and regression, can be applied to train machine learning models on labeled data sets containing examples of normal and malicious activities, enabling organizations to build predictive models that can accurately classify and identify security threats based on observed patterns and characteristics.

CLI commands such as scikit-learn or TensorFlow can be employed to train supervised learning models, such as support vector machines (SVMs) or random forests, on labeled data sets in edge environments, enabling organizations to develop accurate and reliable threat detection algorithms that can effectively distinguish between benign and malicious activities. Unsupervised learning techniques, such as clustering and anomaly detection, can be applied to identify unusual patterns or outliers in data sets without the need for labeled examples, enabling organizations to detect previously unknown or emerging security threats and anomalies in real-time.

CLI commands such as scikit-learn or TensorFlow can be used to train unsupervised learning models, such as k-means clustering or isolation forests, on unlabeled data sets in edge environments, enabling organizations to uncover hidden patterns and anomalies that may indicate a potential security breach or intrusion attempt. Reinforcement learning techniques, such as deep Q-learning, can be applied to develop adaptive and self-learning threat detection systems that can continuously improve and adapt to evolving security threats and attack techniques in dynamic edge environments. CLI commands such as

TensorFlow or Keras can be employed to train reinforcement learning models on simulated environments or historical data sets in edge environments, enabling organizations to develop intelligent threat detection systems that can effectively mitigate security threats and adapt to changing conditions in real-time. By leveraging machine learning-based threat detection techniques at the edge, organizations can enhance their cybersecurity defenses and protect against a wide range of security threats and attack vectors, including malware infections, network intrusions, insider threats, and data breaches.

CLI commands such as scikit-learn or TensorFlow can be used to deploy trained machine learning models in edge environments, enabling organizations to analyze incoming data streams and identify potential security threats and anomalies in real-time, allowing for timely detection and response to security incidents before they can cause harm or damage. In summary, machine learning-based threat detection represents a powerful and versatile approach to enhancing cybersecurity defenses at the edge, enabling organizations to detect and mitigate security threats in real-time and protect against evolving cyber threats and attack techniques in dynamic edge environments. By leveraging advanced machine learning algorithms and techniques, organizations can develop intelligent threat detection systems that can effectively identify and respond to security threats and vulnerabilities, safeguarding their edge deployments and ensuring the integrity, confidentiality, and availability of their data and resources.

Chapter 7: Performance Optimization Techniques

Caching strategies play a vital role in improving the performance and responsiveness of edge computing systems, enabling organizations to efficiently deliver content and services to end-users with reduced latency and network overhead. CLI commands such as Redis or Memcached can be deployed to implement caching solutions in edge environments, enabling organizations to store frequently accessed data and resources closer to the point of consumption, thereby reducing the need to fetch data from distant servers and improving overall system performance. By caching frequently accessed data at the edge, organizations can minimize the latency associated with retrieving data from remote servers, resulting in faster response times and improved user experiences for applications and services deployed in edge environments. CLI commands such as Varnish or Nginx can be employed to configure caching proxies in edge environments, enabling organizations to cache static assets such as images, CSS files, and JavaScript libraries at the edge, reducing the load on origin servers and accelerating content delivery to end-users. Content delivery networks (CDNs) leverage caching techniques to distribute content across a geographically distributed network of edge servers, enabling organizations to deliver content to end-users from the nearest edge location, thereby reducing latency and improving performance. CLI commands such as Cloudflare or Akamai can be utilized to deploy CDNs in edge environments, enabling organizations to cache and deliver static and dynamic content, including web pages, images, videos, and streaming media, with reduced latency and improved reliability. Edge caching can also be applied to cache application data and API responses at the edge, enabling organizations to reduce the round-trip time for requests and improve the responsiveness of applications deployed in edge environments. CLI commands such as Fastly or Amazon CloudFront can be employed to configure edge caching for dynamic content and API responses, enabling organizations to cache frequently accessed data and resources at the edge, thereby reducing the load on backend servers and improving application performance. In addition to improving performance, caching strategies can also help organizations reduce bandwidth consumption and mitigate the impact of network congestion on edge deployments. CLI commands such as Squid or

HAProxy can be used to configure caching reverse proxies in edge environments, enabling organizations to cache HTTP responses and serve cached content to clients, thereby reducing the amount of data transferred over the network and improving overall network efficiency. Edge caching can be further optimized through the use of cache invalidation techniques, enabling organizations to expire or invalidate cached content in response to changes in data or application logic. CLI commands such as purging cache or cache-control headers can be employed to implement cache invalidation strategies in edge environments, enabling organizations to ensure that cached content remains fresh and up-to-date, thereby maintaining data consistency and integrity across edge deployments. By implementing caching strategies in edge environments, organizations can achieve significant performance improvements and deliver faster, more responsive experiences to end-users, thereby enhancing user satisfaction and driving business growth. CLI commands such as varnishadm or curl can be used to monitor and manage caching performance in edge environments, enabling organizations to fine-tune caching configurations and optimize cache hit rates for maximum efficiency and effectiveness. In summary, caching strategies are essential for improving the performance and responsiveness of edge computing systems, enabling organizations to deliver content and services with reduced latency and network overhead, thereby enhancing user experiences and driving business success in the era of edge computing.

Edge computing performance metrics and monitoring are essential aspects of managing and optimizing edge deployments, providing organizations with insights into the health, availability, and efficiency of their edge infrastructure and applications. CLI commands such as Prometheus or Grafana can be deployed to implement performance monitoring solutions in edge environments, enabling organizations to collect, store, and visualize key performance metrics from edge devices, servers, and applications in real-time. Performance monitoring encompasses a wide range of metrics, including latency, throughput, CPU utilization, memory usage, network traffic, and error rates, which are critical for assessing the performance and reliability of edge computing systems. CLI commands such as top or htop can be used to monitor CPU and memory usage on edge devices and servers, providing insights into resource utilization and identifying potential bottlenecks that may impact performance. Latency is a key performance metric for edge computing, measuring the time it takes for data to travel from the source to the destination, including processing and transmission delays. CLI commands such as ping or traceroute can be employed to measure latency between edge devices and servers, enabling organizations to assess network performance and identify latency-sensitive applications and workloads. Throughput refers to the rate at which data is transmitted or processed by edge devices and servers, representing the capacity and efficiency of the edge infrastructure. CLI commands such as iperf or speedtest-cli can be used to measure throughput between edge devices and servers, enabling organizations to assess network bandwidth and optimize data transfer speeds for maximum efficiency. CPU utilization measures the percentage of CPU resources used by edge devices and servers, indicating the level of computational workload and performance capacity available for processing tasks and applications. CLI commands such as mpstat or sar can be employed to monitor CPU utilization in real-time, enabling organizations to identify CPU-intensive tasks and optimize resource allocation for improved performance. Memory usage reflects the amount of RAM consumed by *edge devices and servers, indicating the availability and utilization of memory resources for storing and accessing data and applications. CLI commands such as free or vmstat can be used to monitor memory usage and identify memory-intensive processes or applications that may impact system performance. Network traffic measures the volume of data transmitted between edge devices and servers, representing the workload and demand on the network infrastructure. CLI commands such as ifconfig or netstat can be employed to monitor network traffic in real-time, enabling organizations to identify bandwidth-intensive applications and optimize network performance for improved throughput and responsiveness. Error rates quantify the frequency of errors and failures encountered by edge devices and servers, indicating the reliability and stability of the edge infrastructure and applications. CLI commands such as grep or awk can be used to parse log files and identify error messages and exceptions, enabling organizations to troubleshoot issues and implement corrective actions to improve system reliability and performance. Performance monitoring solutions enable organizations to visualize performance metrics through dashboards and reports, providing actionable insights and alerts to stakeholders and administrators. CLI commands such as curl or wget can be used to retrieve data from monitoring APIs and generate custom reports or notifications based on predefined thresholds and conditions. By monitoring key performance metrics and trends over time, organizations can identify performance bottlenecks, optimize resource allocation, and improve the overall efficiency and reliability of their edge computing deployments. CLI commands such as cron or systemd can be employed to schedule automated monitoring tasks and alerts, enabling organizations to proactively identify and address performance issues before they impact users and applications. In summary, edge computing performance metrics and monitoring are critical for assessing and optimizing the performance, reliability, and efficiency of edge infrastructure and applications, enabling organizations to deliver superior user experiences and drive business success in today's digital landscape.*

Chapter 8: Load Balancing and Resource Management

Dynamic load balancing in edge computing clusters is a critical strategy for optimizing resource utilization, improving performance, and ensuring high availability of services across distributed environments. CLI commands such as HAProxy or Nginx can be deployed to implement dynamic load balancing solutions in edge clusters, enabling organizations to distribute incoming traffic efficiently among edge nodes based on factors such as current load, network conditions, and application-specific requirements. Load balancing algorithms play a key role in determining how traffic is distributed among edge nodes, with various algorithms offering different trade-offs in terms of performance, fairness, and simplicity. CLI commands such as ipvsadm or iptables can be used to configure IP-based load balancing in edge clusters, enabling organizations to route traffic to different edge nodes based on destination IP addresses and load balancing policies. Round-robin is a simple and widely used load balancing algorithm that distributes traffic evenly among edge nodes in a cyclic fashion, *ensuring that each node receives an equal share of requests over time. CLI commands such as sysctl or echo can be employed to adjust kernel parameters and enable round-robin load balancing in edge clusters, enabling organizations to achieve basic load distribution without the need for complex configurations or external components. Weighted round-robin is a variation of the round-robin algorithm that assigns different weights to edge nodes based on their capacity or performance, allowing organizations to allocate more traffic to higher-capacity nodes and less traffic to lower-capacity nodes. CLI commands such as ipvsadm or sysctl can be used to configure weighted round-robin load balancing in edge clusters, enabling organizations to achieve more granular control over traffic distribution and resource utilization. Least connections is a load balancing algorithm that directs incoming traffic to the edge node with the fewest active connections, enabling organizations to distribute traffic based on real-time load conditions and prevent overloading of individual nodes. CLI commands such as iptables or sysctl can be employed to implement least connections load balancing in edge clusters, enabling organizations to optimize resource allocation and improve overall system performance. Source IP hashing is a load* balancing algorithm that uses the source IP address of incoming requests to determine which edge node should handle the traffic, ensuring that requests from the same client are consistently routed to the same node, which can improve caching efficiency and session persistence. CLI commands such as ipvsadm or iptables can be used to configure source IP hashing load balancing in edge clusters, enabling organizations to achieve deterministic routing and maintain session affinity for stateful applications. Dynamic load balancing in edge computing clusters requires continuous monitoring of node performance and network conditions to dynamically adjust traffic distribution and ensure optimal resource utilization. CLI commands such as curl or wget can be employed to retrieve performance metrics and health checks from edge nodes, enabling organizations to make informed decisions about load balancing configurations and adapt to changing workload patterns in real-time. Automation tools such as Ansible or Terraform can be used to deploy and manage load balancing configurations across edge clusters, enabling organizations to automate the provisioning and configuration of load balancing components and streamline the management of distributed environments. By implementing dynamic load *balancing strategies in edge computing clusters, organizations can improve scalability, reliability, and performance of their applications and services, enabling them to meet the growing demands of modern digital experiences and deliver superior user experiences across diverse edge environments.*

Resource allocation algorithms are crucial components of edge resource management systems, responsible for intelligently distributing computing, storage, and network resources among edge devices and applications to maximize efficiency and performance. CLI commands such as Kubernetes or Docker Swarm can be deployed to implement resource allocation algorithms in edge computing environments, enabling organizations to orchestrate and manage containerized workloads across distributed clusters of edge devices. One commonly used resource allocation algorithm in edge computing is the proportional allocation algorithm, which allocates resources to edge devices based on their proportional share of the total capacity, ensuring that each device receives a fair and equitable portion of available resources. CLI commands such as kubectl or docker-compose can be used to define resource constraints and limits for containerized workloads, enabling organizations to enforce resource

215

allocation policies and prevent individual devices from monopolizing resources in edge clusters. Another resource allocation algorithm is the priority-based algorithm, which assigns priorities to different edge devices or applications based on their importance or criticality, allowing higher-priority tasks to receive preferential treatment in resource allocation decisions. CLI commands such as Docker or Kubernetes can be employed to assign priority levels to containerized workloads, enabling organizations to ensure that mission-critical applications receive the necessary resources to meet their performance objectives. Weighted fair queuing is a resource allocation algorithm commonly used in network traffic management, which assigns weights to different traffic flows based on their importance or service level agreements (SLAs), ensuring that higher-priority traffic receives a larger share of available bandwidth and network resources. CLI commands such as tc or iptables can be used to configure weighted fair queuing policies in edge routers or gateways, enabling organizations to prioritize traffic based on application requirements and quality of service (QoS) criteria. Dynamic resource allocation algorithms are designed to adaptively adjust resource allocations based on real-time workload demands and performance metrics, *enabling organizations to optimize resource utilization and responsiveness in dynamic edge environments. CLI commands such as Prometheus or Grafana can be employed to collect and analyze performance metrics from edge devices and applications, enabling organizations to dynamically adjust resource allocations based on workload characteristics and performance requirements. Machine learning algorithms can be leveraged to develop predictive resource allocation models that anticipate future workload demands and adjust resource allocations proactively to prevent performance bottlenecks or resource contention issues. CLI commands such as TensorFlow or PyTorch can be used to train machine learning models on historical performance data and workload patterns, enabling organizations to predict future resource requirements and optimize resource allocations accordingly. Hybrid resource allocation algorithms combine multiple allocation strategies, such as proportional allocation, priority-based allocation, and dynamic allocation, to achieve a balance between fairness, efficiency, and adaptability in edge environments. CLI commands such as kubectl or Docker Swarm can be employed to deploy hybrid resource allocation algorithms in edge clusters, enabling organizations to customize allocation policies and adapt to diverse workload scenarios and application requirements. Resource allocation algorithms play a crucial role in optimizing resource utilization, improving performance, and ensuring reliability in edge computing environments, enabling organizations to maximize the value of their edge infrastructure and deliver superior user experiences across distributed edge applications and services. CLI commands such as Ansible or Puppet can be used to automate the deployment and configuration of resource allocation algorithms in edge clusters, enabling organizations to streamline operations and scale their edge deployments effectively. In summary, resource allocation algorithms are essential for effective resource management in edge computing environments, enabling organizations to allocate resources intelligently, adaptively, and efficiently to meet the demands of modern edge applications and services.*

Chapter 9: Containerization and Orchestration Solutions

Containerization has emerged as a fundamental technology for deploying and managing applications in edge computing environments, offering benefits such as portability, scalability, and resource efficiency. CLI commands such as Docker or Podman can be used to create, manage, and run containers on edge devices, enabling organizations to encapsulate applications and their dependencies into lightweight, isolated containers that can be easily deployed and executed across diverse edge environments. Docker is a leading containerization platform that simplifies the process of building, packaging, and distributing applications as containers, providing developers and operators with a consistent and reliable environment for running their workloads. Kubernetes, on the other hand, is a powerful orchestration platform that automates the deployment, scaling, and management of containerized applications, providing advanced features such as service discovery, load balancing, and automated rollouts to streamline operations in distributed environments. CLI commands such as kubectl or docker-compose can be employed to deploy and manage containerized workloads in edge environments, enabling organizations to leverage the benefits of containerization and orchestration to build resilient and scalable edge applications. One of the key advantages of using Docker for edge containerization is its lightweight and portable nature, allowing developers to package their applications and dependencies into self-contained images that can be easily deployed and executed on edge devices with minimal overhead. Kubernetes complements Docker by providing advanced orchestration capabilities that enable organizations to deploy and manage containerized workloads at scale, ensuring high availability, fault tolerance, and performance optimization in edge environments. Together, Docker and Kubernetes form a powerful stack for edge containerization, enabling organizations to build, deploy, and manage containerized applications across distributed edge clusters with ease. CLI commands such as kubectl apply or docker build can be used to build and deploy containerized applications in Kubernetes clusters, enabling organizations to streamline the deployment process and ensure consistency across edge environments. Containerization with Docker and Kubernetes simplifies the process of *developing and deploying edge applications, enabling organizations to package their applications and dependencies into self-contained units that can be easily distributed and executed across diverse edge environments. CLI commands such as docker push or kubectl create can be employed to distribute container images and deploy applications in edge clusters, enabling organizations to streamline the deployment process and accelerate time-to-market for edge applications. In addition to simplifying deployment, Docker and Kubernetes provide organizations with the flexibility to scale their applications dynamically in response to changing workload demands, enabling them to optimize resource utilization and improve performance in edge environments. CLI commands such as kubectl scale or docker service scale can be used to scale containerized applications horizontally or vertically in Kubernetes or Docker Swarm clusters, enabling organizations to adjust resource allocations and meet fluctuating demand in real-time. By leveraging Docker and Kubernetes for edge containerization, organizations can unlock the full potential of edge computing, enabling them to build and deploy resilient, scalable, and efficient applications that deliver superior performance and reliability in distributed environments.*

Edge orchestration platforms and tools play a crucial role in managing and coordinating edge computing resources and workloads across distributed environments, enabling organizations to deploy, monitor, and manage edge applications effectively. CLI commands such as Ansible or Puppet can be used to automate the deployment and configuration of edge infrastructure and applications, enabling organizations to streamline operations and ensure consistency across edge environments. These platforms and tools provide a centralized management interface that allows administrators to provision and configure edge devices, deploy applications, and monitor performance and resource utilization in real-time. CLI commands such as Docker or Kubernetes can be employed to deploy containerized applications in edge environments, enabling organizations to leverage containerization and orchestration to simplify deployment and improve scalability and reliability. Edge orchestration platforms typically include features such as automated provisioning, configuration management, and monitoring, enabling organizations to manage edge infrastructure and applications efficiently and effectively. CLI commands such as Terraform or CloudFormation can be used to provision and configure edge infrastructure resources, such as virtual machines, containers, and networking components, enabling organizations to automate the deployment and management of edge environments. These platforms and tools enable organizations to abstract the complexity of edge computing infrastructure and provide a unified interface for managing edge resources and applications, enabling administrators to focus on developing and deploying edge applications rather than managing underlying infrastructure. CLI commands such as kubectl or docker-compose can be employed to deploy and manage containerized applications in edge environments, enabling organizations to leverage containerization and orchestration to simplify deployment and improve scalability and reliability. Edge orchestration platforms and tools enable organizations to deploy and manage edge applications across distributed environments, ensuring consistent performance and reliability regardless of location or network conditions. CLI commands such as Ansible or Chef can be used to automate the deployment and configuration of edge devices, enabling organizations to streamline operations and ensure consistency across edge environments. These platforms and tools provide organizations with the flexibility to deploy and manage edge applications on-premises, in the cloud, or at the edge, enabling them to leverage the benefits of edge computing while maintaining control over their infrastructure and data. CLI commands such as Docker or Kubernetes can be employed to deploy containerized applications in edge environments, enabling organizations to leverage containerization and orchestration to simplify deployment and improve scalability and reliability. Edge orchestration platforms and tools provide organizations with the visibility and control they need to manage edge infrastructure and applications effectively, enabling them to optimize performance, reduce costs, and accelerate time-to-market for edge applications and services. CLI commands such as Terraform or CloudFormation can be used to provision and configure edge infrastructure resources, such as virtual machines, containers, and networking components, enabling organizations to automate the deployment and management of edge environments. Overall, edge orchestration platforms and tools are essential for organizations looking to harness the power of edge computing, enabling them to deploy and manage edge applications effectively and efficiently across distributed environments.

Chapter 10: Continuous Improvement and Future Directions

Continuous Integration/Continuous Deployment (CI/CD) has become a cornerstone of modern software development practices, enabling organizations to automate the build, test, and deployment processes to deliver high-quality software quickly and reliably. CLI commands such as Git or SVN can be used to manage source code repositories, enabling developers to collaborate on code changes and track version history efficiently. In the context of edge computing, CI/CD practices are essential for ensuring the seamless deployment and updates of edge applications across distributed environments, where reliability, scalability, and performance are critical. CLI commands such as Jenkins or GitLab CI can be employed to set up CI/CD pipelines for edge applications, enabling organizations to automate the integration, testing, and deployment of code changes to edge devices and clusters. The CI/CD pipeline typically consists of multiple stages, including code compilation, unit testing, integration testing, and deployment, with each stage designed to verify the correctness and quality of the code before it is deployed to production environments. CLI commands such as Docker or Kubernetes can be used to package and deploy containerized applications in edge environments, enabling organizations to leverage containerization and orchestration to streamline deployment and improve scalability and reliability. By automating the deployment process, CI/CD practices reduce the risk of human error and ensure consistent deployments across edge environments, leading to improved reliability and reduced downtime. CLI commands such as Ansible or Puppet can be employed to automate the configuration and provisioning of edge devices, enabling organizations to ensure that edge infrastructure is properly configured and maintained throughout the deployment process. In addition to automating deployment, CI/CD practices enable organizations to implement continuous testing, where code changes are automatically tested against predefined criteria to ensure that they meet quality standards before being deployed to production environments. CLI commands such as Selenium or JUnit can be used to automate unit tests, integration tests, and end-to-end tests for edge applications, enabling organizations to identify and fix issues early in the development process. Continuous monitoring and feedback are integral to CI/CD practices, enabling organizations to collect and analyze data on application performance, resource utilization, and user behavior to identify areas for improvement and optimize deployment processes iteratively. CLI commands such as Prometheus or Grafana can be employed to collect and visualize performance metrics from edge devices and applications, enabling organizations to monitor the health and performance of their edge infrastructure in real-time. By implementing CI/CD practices in edge computing, organizations can accelerate the delivery of new features and updates to edge applications, reduce time-to-market, and improve overall software quality and reliability. CLI commands such as Jenkins or GitLab CI can be used to trigger automated tests and deployments based on code changes, enabling organizations to achieve rapid and reliable deployments in edge environments. In summary, CI/CD practices are essential for enabling organizations to deploy and manage edge applications efficiently and effectively, ensuring that they can deliver high-quality software quickly and reliably to meet the demands of modern edge computing environments. Anticipating future trends and technologies in edge computing is essential for staying ahead in the rapidly evolving landscape of distributed computing. CLI commands such as Terraform or CloudFormation can be used to provision and configure edge infrastructure resources, enabling organizations to automate the deployment and management of edge environments. One of the key trends shaping the future of edge computing is the proliferation of edge devices and sensors, driven by advancements in IoT (Internet of Things) technology and the increasing demand for real-time data processing and analysis at the edge. Organizations are deploying edge devices such as sensors, cameras, and actuators in various industries, including manufacturing, healthcare, transportation, and smart cities, to collect and process data closer to the source, enabling faster decision-making and improved operational efficiency. Another significant trend in edge computing is the convergence of edge and cloud technologies, where organizations are leveraging hybrid and multi-cloud architectures to seamlessly integrate edge and cloud resources and applications, enabling them to distribute workloads across distributed environments based on factors such as latency, bandwidth, and cost. CLI commands such as Docker or Kubernetes can be employed to deploy containerized applications in edge environments, enabling organizations to leverage containerization and orchestration to streamline deployment and improve scalability and reliability. Edge computing is also driving innovation in areas such as edge AI (Artificial Intelligence) and edge analytics, where organizations are deploying machine learning models and analytics algorithms directly on edge devices to process and analyze data in real-time, enabling intelligent decision-making and automation at the edge. CLI commands such as Ansible or Puppet can be employed to automate the configuration and provisioning of edge devices, enabling organizations to ensure that edge infrastructure is properly configured and maintained throughout the deployment process. As edge computing continues to evolve, security and privacy will remain paramount concerns, with organizations investing in technologies such *as secure enclaves, encryption, and blockchain to protect sensitive data and ensure compliance with regulations such as GDPR (General Data Protection Regulation) and HIPAA (Health Insurance Portability and Accountability Act). CLI commands such as Git or SVN can be used to manage source code repositories, enabling developers to collaborate on code changes and track version history efficiently. The emergence of 5G networks is also expected to accelerate the adoption of edge computing, enabling organizations to leverage high-speed, low-latency connectivity to deploy and manage edge applications and services across distributed environments. CLI commands such as Jenkins or GitLab CI can be employed to set up CI/CD pipelines for edge applications, enabling organizations to automate the integration, testing, and deployment of code changes to edge devices and clusters. Edge computing is poised to revolutionize industries such as autonomous vehicles, smart cities, and healthcare, where real-time data processing and analysis are critical for enabling new use cases and services. CLI commands such as Prometheus or Grafana can be employed to collect and visualize performance metrics from edge devices and applications, enabling organizations to monitor the health and performance of their edge infrastructure in real-time. In summary, by anticipating future trends and technologies in edge computing, organizations can prepare themselves to harness the full potential of distributed computing and drive innovation in the digital age.*

BOOK 4
EDGE COMPUTING IN INDUSTRY 4.0
PRACTICAL APPLICATIONS AND FUTURE TRENDS

ROB BOTWRIGHT

Chapter 1: Introduction to Industry 4.0 and Edge Computing

Industry 4.0 represents a transformative paradigm shift in manufacturing, driven by the integration of digital technologies into every aspect of the production process. CLI commands such as Terraform or CloudFormation can be used to provision and configure cloud infrastructure resources, enabling manufacturers to deploy and scale digital manufacturing solutions in a cost-effective and efficient manner. At the heart of Industry 4.0 is the concept of the smart factory, where interconnected machines, sensors, and systems communicate and collaborate autonomously to optimize production processes and improve efficiency. Organizations are leveraging technologies such as IoT (Internet of Things), AI (Artificial Intelligence), and robotics to create intelligent manufacturing systems that can adapt and respond to changing market demands in real-time. CLI commands such as Docker or Kubernetes can be employed to containerize and orchestrate manufacturing applications, enabling organizations to deploy and manage software-defined factories with greater flexibility and agility. One of the key benefits of Industry 4.0 is the ability to collect and analyze vast amounts of data from sensors and machines throughout the production process, enabling manufacturers to gain insights into operations, identify inefficiencies, and optimize workflows for maximum productivity and quality. CLI commands such as Git or SVN can be used to manage source code repositories for manufacturing applications, enabling developers to collaborate on code changes and track version history efficiently. With the rise of connected devices and IoT sensors, manufacturers can monitor equipment health and performance in real-time, enabling predictive maintenance and reducing unplanned downtime. CLI commands such as Ansible or Puppet can be employed to automate the configuration and provisioning of manufacturing equipment and systems, enabling organizations to ensure consistency and reliability across their production facilities. Industry 4.0 also enables manufacturers to personalize products and services for individual customers through mass customization, leveraging technologies such as 3D printing and advanced robotics to produce customized products at scale. CLI commands such as Jenkins or GitLab CI can be used to set up continuous integration and deployment pipelines for manufacturing software, enabling organizations to streamline development and deployment processes for improved efficiency and quality. As manufacturers adopt Industry 4.0 technologies, they are also embracing new business models and revenue streams, such as servitization, where companies sell outcomes or services rather than products, and subscription-based pricing models for software and services. CLI commands such as Prometheus or Grafana can be employed to collect and visualize performance metrics from manufacturing equipment and systems, enabling organizations to monitor and optimize production processes in real-time. Industry 4.0 is not just about technology; it requires a cultural shift within organizations to embrace digital transformation and empower employees to leverage new tools and processes to drive innovation and improve competitiveness. In summary, Industry 4.0 is revolutionizing manufacturing by harnessing the power of digital technologies to create smarter, more efficient, and more responsive production *systems that can meet the demands of today's fast-paced global economy. Edge computing plays a pivotal role in Industry 4.0 by extending the capabilities of traditional cloud computing to the edge of the network, enabling real-time data processing and analysis closer to the data source. CLI commands such as Docker or Kubernetes can be employed to deploy edge computing infrastructure, enabling organizations to distribute computing resources and applications across distributed environments for improved performance and efficiency. In the context of Industry 4.0, edge computing enables manufacturers to deploy intelligent manufacturing systems that can collect, process, and analyze data from sensors and machines in real-time, enabling predictive maintenance, quality control, and process optimization. CLI commands such as Ansible or Puppet can be used to automate the configuration and provisioning of edge devices and sensors, enabling organizations to ensure consistency and reliability across their edge deployments. By deploying edge computing solutions, manufacturers can reduce latency and bandwidth constraints, enabling faster decision-making and improved responsiveness in critical* production processes. CLI commands such as Git or SVN can be used to manage edge application code repositories, enabling developers to collaborate on code changes and track version history efficiently. Edge computing also enhances data security and privacy by enabling sensitive data to be processed and analyzed locally, reducing the risk of data breaches and ensuring compliance with regulations such as GDPR and HIPAA. CLI commands such as Terraform or CloudFormation can be employed to provision and manage edge computing resources in a scalable and cost-effective manner, enabling organizations to deploy edge solutions quickly and efficiently. In addition to manufacturing, edge computing has applications across various industries, including healthcare, transportation, energy, and smart cities, where real-time data processing and analysis are critical for enabling new use cases and services. CLI commands such as Jenkins or GitLab CI can be used to set up continuous integration and deployment pipelines for edge applications, enabling organizations to automate the deployment and testing of code changes in edge environments. Edge computing is driving innovation in areas such as autonomous *vehicles, remote patient monitoring, and predictive maintenance, where real-time data processing and analysis are essential for enabling new capabilities and services. CLI commands such as Prometheus or Grafana can be employed to collect and visualize performance metrics from edge devices and applications, enabling organizations to monitor the health and performance of their edge infrastructure in real-time. As organizations continue to adopt Industry 4.0 principles and technologies, edge computing will play an increasingly important role in enabling new use cases and applications that require low-latency, high-throughput data processing and analysis at the edge of the network. In summary, understanding the role of edge computing in Industry 4.0 is essential for organizations seeking to harness the full potential of digital transformation and drive innovation in the digital age.*

Chapter 2: Real-time Data Processing in Manufacturing

Edge computing is revolutionizing manufacturing operations by enabling real-time data processing at the edge of the network, transforming traditional production processes and driving efficiencies across the supply chain. CLI commands such as Docker or Kubernetes can be employed to deploy edge computing infrastructure within manufacturing facilities, enabling organizations to process and analyze data closer to the source for faster insights and decision-making. In manufacturing, real-time data processing is essential for optimizing production processes, improving quality control, and reducing downtime, as even small delays in data transmission can impact productivity and profitability. CLI commands such as Ansible or Puppet can be used to automate the configuration and provisioning of edge devices and sensors, ensuring consistency and reliability in data collection and analysis. By deploying edge computing solutions, manufacturers can overcome latency and bandwidth constraints associated with traditional cloud computing, enabling them to process and analyze data in real-time without relying on centralized data centers. CLI commands such as Git or SVN can be employed to manage edge application code repositories, enabling developers to collaborate on code changes and track version history efficiently. Edge computing also enhances data security in manufacturing operations by enabling sensitive data to be processed and analyzed locally, reducing the risk of data breaches and ensuring compliance with industry regulations. CLI commands such as Terraform or CloudFormation can be used to provision and manage edge computing resources, enabling organizations to scale their edge deployments as needed and adapt to changing production requirements. In addition to improving operational efficiency, edge computing enables manufacturers to unlock new capabilities and services, such as predictive maintenance, remote monitoring, and augmented reality-based training, that can drive innovation and competitive advantage. CLI commands such as Jenkins or GitLab CI can be employed to set up continuous integration and deployment pipelines for edge applications, enabling organizations to automate the deployment and testing of code changes in manufacturing environments. By leveraging edge computing for real-time data processing, manufacturers can gain deeper insights into their operations, optimize production processes, and deliver higher-quality products to market faster than ever before. CLI commands such as Prometheus or Grafana can be employed to collect and visualize performance metrics from edge devices and applications, enabling organizations to monitor the health and performance of their manufacturing operations in real-time. As manufacturing becomes increasingly digitized and connected, edge computing will play an increasingly important role in driving innovation and enabling new use cases and services that improve efficiency, quality, and competitiveness. In summary, leveraging edge computing for real-time data processing in manufacturing operations is essential for organizations seeking to stay ahead in today's rapidly evolving digital landscape.

Case studies provide valuable insights into how real-time data processing is implemented in manufacturing environments, showcasing the benefits and challenges faced by organizations in deploying edge computing solutions. CLI commands such as Docker or Kubernetes can be utilized to deploy edge computing infrastructure within manufacturing facilities, allowing organizations to process data closer to the source for faster insights and decision-making. One notable case study is that of a leading automotive manufacturer that implemented edge computing to monitor and analyze machine data in real-time, enabling predictive maintenance and reducing downtime. The manufacturer used CLI commands such as Ansible or Puppet to automate the configuration and provisioning of edge devices, ensuring consistency and reliability in data collection and analysis across its production facilities. Another case study involves a multinational electronics company that leveraged edge computing to optimize its manufacturing processes, improving efficiency and reducing waste. The company employed CLI commands such as Git or SVN to manage edge application code repositories, enabling developers to collaborate on code changes and track version history efficiently. Additionally, a food and beverage company implemented edge computing to monitor and control its production lines, ensuring product quality and regulatory compliance. The company used CLI commands such as Terraform or CloudFormation to provision and manage edge computing resources, scaling its deployments as needed to meet changing production demands. Furthermore, a pharmaceutical manufacturer utilized edge computing to analyze data from its manufacturing equipment in real-time, enabling proactive maintenance and ensuring product quality and safety. The manufacturer employed CLI commands such as Jenkins or GitLab CI to set up continuous integration and deployment pipelines for its edge applications, automating the deployment and testing of code changes in its manufacturing environments. Additionally, a semiconductor manufacturer implemented edge computing to optimize its production processes, improving yield and reducing time-to-market for its products. The manufacturer used CLI commands such as Prometheus or Grafana to collect and visualize performance metrics from its edge devices and applications, monitoring the health and performance of its manufacturing operations in real-time. These case studies highlight the diverse applications of real-time data processing in manufacturing environments and demonstrate the significant impact that *edge computing can have on operational efficiency, product quality, and competitiveness. As organizations continue to digitize and modernize their manufacturing operations, edge computing will play an increasingly important role in enabling new use cases and driving innovation in the industry.*

Chapter 3: Predictive Maintenance and Condition Monitoring

Predictive maintenance is a proactive approach to maintenance that uses data analytics and machine learning algorithms to predict when equipment is likely to fail, allowing organizations to schedule maintenance before breakdowns occur. CLI commands such as Docker or Kubernetes can be employed to deploy edge computing infrastructure within industrial facilities, enabling real-time data processing and analysis for predictive maintenance applications. By leveraging edge computing, organizations can process data from sensors and machines in real-time, enabling predictive maintenance models to analyze equipment health and performance continuously. CLI commands such as Ansible or Puppet can be used to automate the configuration and provisioning of edge devices, ensuring consistency and reliability in data collection and analysis across manufacturing environments. Predictive maintenance relies on the collection of data from sensors and IoT devices installed on equipment, such as temperature, pressure, vibration, and other performance metrics. CLI commands such as Git or SVN can be employed to manage edge application code repositories, enabling developers to collaborate on code changes and track version history efficiently. This data is then analyzed using machine learning algorithms to identify patterns and anomalies that may indicate impending equipment failure. CLI commands such as Terraform or CloudFormation can be used to provision and manage edge computing resources, scaling deployments as needed to meet changing maintenance requirements. Predictive maintenance can help organizations reduce downtime, improve equipment reliability, and extend asset lifecycles by identifying and addressing potential issues before they lead to costly breakdowns. CLI commands such as Jenkins or GitLab CI can be employed to set up continuous integration and deployment pipelines for predictive maintenance applications, automating the deployment and testing of code changes in industrial environments. By implementing predictive maintenance with edge computing, organizations can optimize their maintenance schedules, reduce maintenance *costs, and minimize unplanned downtime, leading to increased operational efficiency and productivity. CLI commands such as Prometheus or Grafana can be employed to collect and visualize performance metrics from edge devices and applications, enabling organizations to monitor the health and performance of their industrial equipment in real-time. Overall, predictive maintenance with edge computing offers significant benefits for organizations across various industries, enabling them to transition from reactive to proactive maintenance strategies and unlock new levels of efficiency and reliability in their operations. Condition monitoring techniques are essential for ensuring the optimal performance and reliability of industrial equipment, enabling organizations to detect potential issues early and prevent costly downtime. CLI commands such as Docker or Kubernetes can be used to deploy edge computing infrastructure within industrial facilities, facilitating real-time data processing and analysis for condition monitoring applications. One commonly used condition monitoring technique is vibration analysis, which involves measuring and analyzing the vibrations of machinery to detect abnormalities that may* indicate mechanical wear or misalignment. CLI commands such as Ansible or Puppet can automate the configuration and provisioning of edge devices, ensuring consistent and reliable data collection and analysis across manufacturing environments. Another effective technique is thermal imaging, which uses infrared cameras to detect changes in temperature that may indicate overheating or other issues with equipment components. CLI commands such as Git or SVN can manage edge application code repositories, allowing developers to collaborate on code changes and track version history efficiently. Additionally, oil analysis is often used to monitor the condition of lubricants and detect signs of contamination or degradation that could lead to equipment failure. CLI commands such as Terraform or CloudFormation can provision and manage edge computing resources, scaling deployments as needed to accommodate changing monitoring requirements. Ultrasonic testing is another valuable technique for condition monitoring, involving the use of ultrasonic waves to detect flaws or defects in equipment components such as bearings or welds. CLI commands such as Jenkins or GitLab CI can set up continuous *integration and deployment pipelines for condition monitoring applications, automating deployment and testing in industrial environments. By implementing condition monitoring techniques with edge computing, organizations can gain real-time insights into the health and performance of their equipment, enabling proactive maintenance and minimizing downtime. CLI commands such as Prometheus or Grafana can collect and visualize performance metrics from edge devices and applications, allowing organizations to monitor equipment health and performance in real-time. Overall, condition monitoring techniques play a crucial role in ensuring the reliability and efficiency of industrial equipment, helping organizations maximize productivity and minimize maintenance costs.*

Chapter 4: Supply Chain Optimization with Edge Computing

Enhancing supply chain efficiency is a critical goal for organizations seeking to optimize their operations and improve customer satisfaction. CLI commands such as Docker or Kubernetes can be utilized to deploy edge computing infrastructure within supply chain networks, facilitating real-time data processing and analysis for improved efficiency. By leveraging edge computing, organizations can process data closer to the source, enabling faster decision-making and reducing latency in supply chain operations. CLI commands such as Ansible or Puppet can automate the configuration and provisioning of edge devices, ensuring consistency and reliability in data collection and analysis across supply chain nodes. One way edge computing enhances supply chain efficiency is by enabling real-time tracking and monitoring of goods in transit, allowing organizations to identify and address potential issues such as delays or disruptions promptly. CLI commands such as Git or SVN can manage edge application code repositories, enabling developers to collaborate on code changes and track version history efficiently. Additionally, edge computing can facilitate predictive analytics in supply chain management, allowing organizations to anticipate demand fluctuations and optimize inventory levels accordingly. CLI commands such as Terraform or CloudFormation can provision and manage edge computing resources, scaling deployments as needed to accommodate changing supply chain requirements. Another benefit of edge computing in supply chain management is the ability to improve visibility and traceability throughout the supply chain, enabling organizations to track the movement of goods from production to delivery more accurately. CLI commands such as Jenkins or GitLab CI can set up continuous integration and deployment pipelines for supply chain applications, automating deployment and testing in distributed environments. By deploying edge computing solutions, organizations can also enhance security and compliance in their supply chains by implementing real-time monitoring and anomaly detection capabilities. CLI commands such as Prometheus or Grafana can collect and visualize performance metrics from edge devices and applications, allowing organizations to monitor supply chain operations in real-time and identify areas for optimization. Overall, edge computing offers significant opportunities for enhancing supply chain efficiency by enabling real-time data processing, predictive analytics, and improved visibility and traceability throughout the supply chain network. Real-world examples demonstrate the tangible benefits of leveraging edge technologies for supply chain optimization, showcasing how organizations can enhance efficiency, reduce costs, and improve customer satisfaction. CLI commands such as Docker or Kubernetes can be used to deploy edge computing infrastructure within supply chain networks, facilitating real-time data processing and analysis for optimized operations. One notable example is the use of edge computing in inventory management, where sensors and IoT devices deployed in warehouses continuously monitor inventory levels and send real-time updates to a centralized system. CLI commands such as Ansible or Puppet can automate the configuration and provisioning of edge devices, ensuring consistency and reliability in data collection and analysis across supply chain nodes. This enables organizations to maintain optimal inventory levels, reduce stockouts, and minimize excess inventory, leading to improved supply chain efficiency and cost savings. Another example is the application of edge computing in fleet management, where GPS and telematics data from vehicles are processed locally at the edge to provide real-time insights into driver behavior, vehicle performance, and route optimization. CLI commands such as Git or SVN can manage edge application code repositories, enabling developers to collaborate on code changes and track version history efficiently. By analyzing this data in real-time, organizations can optimize delivery routes, reduce fuel consumption, and improve overall fleet efficiency. Additionally, edge computing is being increasingly used in demand forecasting and predictive analytics, where machine learning algorithms analyze historical sales data, market trends, and external factors to predict future demand more accurately. CLI commands such as Terraform or CloudFormation can provision and manage edge computing resources, scaling deployments as needed to accommodate changing supply chain requirements. By *leveraging edge technologies for demand forecasting, organizations can minimize stockouts, reduce excess inventory, and improve inventory turnover rates, leading to increased profitability and customer satisfaction. Furthermore, edge computing is revolutionizing last-mile delivery operations, where drones and autonomous vehicles equipped with edge computing capabilities can deliver packages more efficiently and cost-effectively. CLI commands such as Jenkins or GitLab CI can set up continuous integration and deployment pipelines for supply chain applications, automating deployment and testing in distributed environments. By processing data locally at the edge, these delivery vehicles can navigate obstacles, avoid traffic congestion, and make real-time decisions to optimize delivery routes and schedules. In summary, real-world examples highlight the transformative impact of edge technologies on supply chain optimization, demonstrating how organizations can leverage these technologies to streamline operations, reduce costs, and deliver superior customer experiences.*

Chapter 5: Edge Computing in Smart Cities and Infrastructure

Transforming urban infrastructure with edge computing presents a transformative approach to addressing the complex challenges faced by modern cities, leveraging advanced technologies to enhance efficiency, sustainability, and livability. CLI commands such as Docker or Kubernetes can be utilized to deploy edge computing infrastructure within urban environments, facilitating real-time data processing and analysis for improved operations. One key area where edge computing is making a significant impact is in the development of smart transportation systems, where sensors and IoT devices deployed throughout the city gather data on traffic patterns, public transportation usage, and road conditions. CLI commands such as Ansible or Puppet can automate the configuration and provisioning of edge devices, ensuring consistency and reliability in data collection and analysis across urban nodes. By processing this data at the edge, cities can optimize traffic flow, reduce congestion, and improve the overall efficiency of their transportation networks. Additionally, edge computing plays a vital role in enhancing public safety and security in urban areas, where video surveillance cameras equipped with edge computing capabilities can analyze live video feeds in real-time to detect and respond to security threats or emergencies. CLI commands such as Git or SVN can manage edge application code repositories, enabling developers to collaborate on code changes and track version history efficiently. This enables authorities to deploy resources more effectively, improve incident response times, and enhance overall safety for residents and visitors. Furthermore, edge computing is revolutionizing the management of urban utilities such as water, electricity, and waste management, where sensors and actuators deployed throughout the city monitor infrastructure performance and consumption patterns. CLI commands such as Terraform or CloudFormation can provision and manage edge computing resources, scaling deployments as needed to accommodate changing urban infrastructure requirements. By analyzing this data at the edge, cities can optimize resource allocation, reduce waste, and improve the sustainability of their utility systems. Moreover, edge computing enables the development of smart buildings and infrastructure, where sensors and automation systems optimize energy usage, lighting, and HVAC systems based on real-time occupancy and environmental conditions. CLI commands such as Jenkins or GitLab CI can set up continuous integration and deployment pipelines for urban infrastructure applications, automating deployment and testing in distributed environments. By leveraging edge computing, cities can reduce energy consumption, lower operating costs, and create more comfortable and efficient living and working environments for residents. In summary, transforming urban infrastructure with edge computing offers cities a powerful tool for addressing complex challenges and creating more sustainable, resilient, and livable environments for all. Smart city initiatives represent a concerted effort by urban authorities to leverage technology and data-driven approaches to address the diverse needs of modern urban environments, and edge computing plays a crucial role in enabling the realization of these initiatives. CLI commands such as Docker or Kubernetes can be used to deploy edge computing infrastructure within smart city environments, facilitating real-time data processing and analysis for improved urban services. One of the key applications of edge computing in smart cities is in the realm of urban mobility, where sensors and IoT devices deployed throughout the city gather data on traffic flow, public transportation usage, and parking availability. CLI commands such as Ansible or Puppet can automate the configuration and provisioning of edge devices, ensuring consistency and reliability in data collection and analysis across urban nodes. By processing this data at the edge, cities can optimize traffic management, reduce congestion, and enhance the overall efficiency of their transportation networks. Additionally, edge computing is instrumental in enhancing public safety and security within smart cities, where surveillance cameras equipped with edge computing capabilities can analyze live video feeds to detect and respond to security threats or emergencies in real-time. CLI commands such as Git or SVN can manage edge application code repositories, enabling developers to collaborate on code changes and track version history efficiently. This enables authorities to deploy resources more *effectively, improve incident response times, and enhance overall safety for residents and visitors. Furthermore, edge computing is revolutionizing the management of urban utilities such as water, electricity, and waste management, where sensors and actuators deployed throughout the city monitor infrastructure performance and consumption patterns. CLI commands such as Terraform or CloudFormation can provision and manage edge computing resources, scaling deployments as needed to accommodate changing urban infrastructure requirements. By analyzing this data at the edge, cities can optimize resource allocation, reduce waste, and improve the sustainability of their utility systems. Moreover, edge computing enables the development of smart buildings and infrastructure, where sensors and automation systems optimize energy usage, lighting, and HVAC systems based on real-time occupancy and environmental conditions. CLI commands such as Jenkins or GitLab CI can set up continuous integration and deployment pipelines for smart city applications, automating deployment and testing in distributed environments. By leveraging edge computing, cities can reduce energy consumption, lower operating costs, and create more comfortable and efficient living and working environments for residents. In summary, smart city initiatives harness the power of edge computing to address the complex challenges faced by urban environments, paving the way for more sustainable, resilient, and livable cities of the future.*

Chapter 6: Edge Analytics for Enhanced Decision-Making

Harnessing edge analytics for data-driven decision-making represents a paradigm shift in how organizations leverage data to gain insights and drive business outcomes, and deploying edge analytics solutions often involves utilizing various CLI commands to manage and configure the underlying infrastructure. One of the key advantages of edge analytics is its ability to process and analyze data closer to the source, reducing latency and enabling real-time decision-making in distributed environments.

CLI commands such as Docker or Kubernetes can be used to deploy edge analytics applications on distributed edge nodes, allowing organizations to process data at the edge and derive actionable insights without the need to transmit large volumes of data to centralized data centers. By analyzing data at the edge, organizations can gain valuable insights into the performance of IoT devices, machinery, and equipment in industrial settings, enabling predictive maintenance and optimization of operational processes. CLI commands such as Ansible or Puppet can automate the deployment and management of edge analytics software stacks, ensuring consistency and reliability across distributed edge environments. Additionally, edge analytics enables organizations to derive insights from data generated by sensors, cameras, and other IoT devices deployed in smart city environments, facilitating better urban planning, traffic management, and public safety initiatives. CLI commands such as Git or SVN can be used to version control edge analytics application code, enabling collaboration among data scientists and developers working on analytics models and algorithms.

This allows organizations to iteratively improve and refine their edge analytics solutions over time. Furthermore, edge analytics is instrumental in enabling real-time monitoring and analysis of data in healthcare settings, where wearable devices, patient monitors, and medical equipment generate vast amounts of data that can be analyzed at the point of care to improve patient outcomes. CLI commands such as Terraform or CloudFormation can automate the provisioning and configuration of edge analytics infrastructure, allowing healthcare organizations to quickly deploy and scale analytics solutions to support their operations. Moreover, edge analytics plays a crucial role in enhancing the performance of retail operations, where real-time analysis of customer data, inventory levels, and sales trends can inform pricing strategies, promotional campaigns, and inventory management decisions. CLI commands such as Jenkins or GitLab CI can set up continuous integration and deployment pipelines for edge analytics applications, enabling organizations to streamline the development and deployment process.

By harnessing edge analytics, organizations can unlock the full potential of their data assets, gaining insights and intelligence that drive innovation, efficiency, and competitive advantage in today's fast-paced digital economy. In summary, edge analytics represents a powerful approach to data-driven decision-making, enabling organizations to derive insights and intelligence from data at the edge of the network, where it is generated, to drive better *business outcomes and improve operational efficiency across a wide range of industries and use cases.*

Real-time insights provided by edge analytics empower decision-makers with timely and relevant information to drive strategic actions and operational decisions, and deploying edge analytics solutions often involves utilizing various CLI commands to manage and configure the underlying infrastructure. One of the key advantages of edge analytics is its ability to process and analyze data closer to the point of generation, reducing latency and enabling rapid decision-making in distributed environments. CLI commands such as Docker or Kubernetes can be used to deploy edge analytics applications on distributed edge nodes, allowing organizations to process data in real-time and derive actionable insights without the need to transmit large volumes of data to centralized data centers. By analyzing data at the edge, decision-makers can gain valuable insights into the performance of critical assets and processes, enabling proactive maintenance and optimization to minimize downtime and maximize efficiency.

CLI commands such as Ansible or Puppet can automate the deployment and management of edge analytics software stacks, ensuring consistency and reliability across distributed edge environments. Additionally, edge analytics empowers decision-makers with the ability to monitor and respond to events and anomalies in real-time, enabling faster detection and resolution of issues before they escalate into larger problems. CLI commands such as Git or SVN can be used to version control edge analytics application code, facilitating collaboration among data scientists and developers working on analytics models and algorithms.

This allows decision-makers to iteratively refine their analytics solutions and adapt to changing business needs and requirements. Furthermore, edge analytics enables decision-makers to leverage machine learning and AI algorithms to uncover hidden patterns and correlations in data, enabling predictive and prescriptive analytics to drive informed decision-making. CLI commands such as Terraform or CloudFormation can automate the provisioning and configuration of edge analytics infrastructure, allowing *organizations to quickly deploy and scale analytics solutions to support their operations. Moreover, real-time insights provided by edge analytics empower decision-makers across a wide range of industries and use cases, from manufacturing and supply chain management to healthcare and retail. CLI commands such as Jenkins or GitLab CI can set up continuous integration and deployment pipelines for edge analytics applications, streamlining the development and deployment process. By harnessing the power of edge analytics, decision-makers can make faster, more informed decisions that drive business growth, improve operational efficiency, and enhance customer experiences. In summary, real-time insights provided by edge analytics are transforming decision-making processes, enabling organizations to stay ahead of the competition and thrive in today's fast-paced, data-driven world.*

Chapter 7: Edge Computing in Healthcare and Telemedicine

Advancements in healthcare delivery through edge computing have revolutionized the industry by enabling faster and more efficient access to critical patient data and medical services, and deploying edge computing solutions often involves utilizing various CLI commands to manage and configure the underlying infrastructure. One of the key advantages of edge computing in healthcare is its ability to process and analyze patient data closer to the point of care, reducing latency and enabling real-time decision-making by healthcare providers. CLI commands such as Docker or Kubernetes can be used to deploy edge computing applications on distributed edge nodes within healthcare facilities, allowing for rapid processing and analysis of patient data without relying on centralized data centers. By leveraging edge computing, healthcare providers can improve the delivery of medical services, such as telemedicine and remote patient monitoring, by ensuring timely access to patient data and enabling virtual consultations and diagnostics in real-time. CLI commands such as Ansible or Puppet can automate the deployment and management of edge computing software stacks, ensuring consistency and reliability across distributed healthcare environments. Additionally, edge computing enables healthcare organizations to enhance patient outcomes through personalized and proactive care delivery, leveraging data analytics and machine learning algorithms to identify trends and patterns in patient data and predict health risks or potential medical emergencies. CLI commands such as Git or SVN can be used to version control edge computing application code, facilitating collaboration among healthcare professionals and data scientists working on analytics models and algorithms to improve patient care. This allows healthcare providers to tailor treatment plans and interventions to individual patient needs, ultimately leading to better health outcomes and improved patient satisfaction. Furthermore, edge computing plays a crucial role in supporting the Internet of Medical Things (IoMT) ecosystem, which includes wearable devices, remote monitoring sensors, and medical equipment connected to the internet to collect *and transmit patient data. CLI commands such as Terraform or CloudFormation can automate the provisioning and configuration of edge computing infrastructure, allowing healthcare organizations to quickly deploy and scale IoMT solutions to support their operations. Moreover, edge computing enhances the security and privacy of patient data by minimizing the need to transmit sensitive information over public networks, reducing the risk of data breaches and unauthorized access to medical records. CLI commands such as Jenkins or GitLab CI can set up continuous integration and deployment pipelines for edge computing applications, streamlining the development and deployment process in healthcare settings. By embracing edge computing, healthcare organizations can transform the delivery of medical services, improve patient outcomes, and drive innovation in the healthcare industry. In summary, advancements in healthcare delivery through edge computing are enabling healthcare providers to deliver high-quality care more efficiently, effectively, and securely, ultimately benefiting patients and healthcare professionals alike.*

Telemedicine solutions, powered by edge technologies, are transforming the healthcare landscape by enabling remote care delivery to patients wherever they are located, and deploying telemedicine solutions often involves utilizing various CLI commands to manage and configure the underlying infrastructure. One of the key advantages of telemedicine powered by edge technologies is its ability to provide real-time access to medical services and expertise, allowing patients to receive timely consultations and treatment without the need for physical visits to healthcare facilities. CLI commands such as Docker or Kubernetes can be used to deploy telemedicine applications on distributed edge nodes, enabling healthcare providers to deliver virtual consultations and diagnostics efficiently and securely. By leveraging edge technologies, telemedicine solutions overcome geographical barriers and improve healthcare accessibility, particularly for patients in rural or underserved areas with limited access to traditional healthcare services. CLI commands such as Ansible or Puppet can automate the deployment and management of telemedicine software stacks, ensuring seamless and reliable operation across distributed telemedicine networks. Additionally, telemedicine powered by edge technologies enhances patient engagement and empowerment by enabling self-monitoring and management of chronic conditions through remote monitoring devices and mobile health apps. CLI commands such as Git or SVN can be used to version control telemedicine application code, facilitating collaboration among healthcare professionals and software developers to continuously improve telemedicine services and features. This collaborative approach enables the rapid development and deployment of telemedicine solutions that meet the evolving needs of patients and healthcare providers alike. Furthermore, telemedicine solutions leverage edge technologies to ensure high-quality and secure transmission of patient data, protecting sensitive health information from unauthorized access and ensuring compliance with privacy regulations such as HIPAA. CLI commands such as Terraform or CloudFormation can automate the provisioning and configuration of telemedicine infrastructure, enabling healthcare organizations to scale their telemedicine services to meet growing demand and serve a larger patient population. Moreover, *telemedicine powered by edge technologies enables healthcare providers to deliver personalized and proactive care by leveraging data analytics and artificial intelligence algorithms to analyze patient data and identify trends or patterns that may indicate health risks or treatment opportunities. CLI commands such as Jenkins or GitLab CI can set up continuous integration and deployment pipelines for telemedicine applications, streamlining the development and deployment process and ensuring the rapid rollout of new features and updates. By embracing telemedicine solutions powered by edge technologies, healthcare organizations can enhance patient outcomes, improve healthcare access and affordability, and drive innovation in the delivery of medical services. In summary, telemedicine solutions enabled by edge technologies are revolutionizing healthcare delivery by providing convenient, accessible, and personalized care to patients regardless of their location, ultimately improving health outcomes and enhancing the patient experience.*

Chapter 8: Regulatory and Compliance Considerations

Navigating regulatory challenges in Industry 4.0 and edge computing involves understanding and adhering to a complex web of laws, regulations, and standards that govern various aspects of technology adoption and deployment, and compliance with these regulations is crucial for businesses to avoid legal liabilities and reputational damage. CLI commands such as compliance check scripts can be used to assess whether an organization's technology infrastructure complies with relevant regulations and standards, helping identify areas that require remediation or improvement. One of the key regulatory challenges in Industry 4.0 and edge computing is data privacy and protection, with regulations such as the General Data Protection Regulation (GDPR) in the European Union and the California Consumer Privacy Act (CCPA) in the United States imposing strict requirements on how organizations collect, store, and process personal data. Deploying techniques such as data encryption and anonymization can help organizations comply with data privacy regulations, ensuring that sensitive information is adequately protected against unauthorized access or disclosure. Another regulatory challenge in Industry 4.0 and edge computing is cybersecurity, with regulations such as the NIST Cybersecurity Framework and the EU Cybersecurity Act setting standards for securing critical infrastructure and protecting against cyber threats. CLI commands such as vulnerability scanning tools can be used to assess the security posture of edge computing systems and identify potential vulnerabilities that need to be addressed to comply with cybersecurity regulations.

Additionally, regulations such as the Federal Information Security Management Act (FISMA) in the United States require government agencies to implement robust cybersecurity measures to protect sensitive information and ensure the integrity and availability of their systems and data. Deploying techniques such as network segmentation and access controls can help government agencies comply with FISMA requirements, limiting the exposure of critical assets to unauthorized users and minimizing the *impact of security incidents. Moreover, regulatory compliance in Industry 4.0 and edge computing extends beyond data privacy and cybersecurity to encompass other areas such as product safety, environmental protection, and intellectual property rights. CLI commands such as configuration management tools can help organizations maintain compliance with regulatory requirements by ensuring that their technology systems are configured and operated in accordance with industry best practices and legal standards. Furthermore, regulatory compliance in Industry 4.0 and edge computing often requires organizations to implement robust governance and risk management processes to identify, assess, and mitigate regulatory risks effectively.*

Deploying techniques such as risk assessment frameworks and audit trails can help organizations demonstrate compliance with regulatory requirements and provide assurance to regulators and stakeholders that they are managing regulatory risks effectively. Additionally, regulatory compliance in Industry 4.0 and edge computing requires organizations to stay abreast of changes in laws, regulations, and standards that may impact their operations and adapt their practices accordingly. CLI commands such as compliance monitoring tools can help organizations track changes in regulatory requirements and assess their implications for their technology infrastructure, enabling them to make informed decisions and take proactive steps to maintain compliance. In summary, navigating regulatory challenges in Industry 4.0 and edge computing requires organizations to adopt a proactive and comprehensive approach to compliance that encompasses data privacy, cybersecurity, product safety, environmental protection, and other regulatory domains. By deploying appropriate techniques and leveraging CLI commands to automate compliance processes, organizations can ensure that they meet regulatory requirements and mitigate legal and reputational risks associated with non-compliance.

Compliance frameworks for edge computing implementations are essential tools that help organizations ensure that their deployments adhere to relevant laws, regulations, and industry standards, and understanding these *frameworks is crucial for organizations seeking to mitigate legal and regulatory risks associated with edge computing initiatives. One widely used compliance framework is the General Data Protection Regulation (GDPR), which governs the processing of personal data of individuals within the European Union and imposes strict requirements on organizations regarding data privacy and security, with CLI commands such as data encryption tools helping organizations achieve compliance with GDPR requirements by protecting sensitive data from unauthorized access or disclosure.*

Another prominent compliance framework is the Health Insurance Portability and Accountability Act (HIPAA), which sets standards for protecting sensitive healthcare information and requires organizations handling healthcare data to implement robust security measures, with techniques such as access controls and audit logging helping healthcare organizations comply with HIPAA regulations by ensuring the confidentiality, integrity, and availability of patient data. Additionally, the Payment Card Industry Data Security Standard (PCI DSS) is a compliance framework that applies to organizations that handle credit card payments, requiring them to implement measures to protect cardholder data and secure payment transactions, and CLI commands such as vulnerability scanning tools can help organizations assess their compliance with PCI DSS requirements by identifying and addressing security vulnerabilities in their payment processing systems. Furthermore, the National Institute of Standards and Technology (NIST) Cybersecurity Framework is a widely recognized cybersecurity framework that provides guidance on managing cybersecurity risks and improving cybersecurity posture, with techniques such as risk assessment tools helping organizations align their cybersecurity practices with NIST framework recommendations and identify areas for improvement in their security programs.

Moreover, industry-specific compliance frameworks such as the Federal Information Security Management Act (FISMA) for government agencies and the Sarbanes-Oxley Act (SOX) for publicly traded companies impose additional requirements on organizations operating in specific sectors, with CLI commands such as configuration management tools assisting organizations in maintaining compliance with FISMA and SOX regulations by ensuring the integrity and confidentiality of sensitive information and providing an audit trail of system changes. Additionally, international standards such as ISO 27001 for information security management and ISO 22301 for business continuity management provide comprehensive frameworks for organizations to establish, implement, maintain, and continually improve their compliance programs, with techniques such as policy management tools helping organizations demonstrate compliance with ISO standards by documenting their policies, procedures, and controls. Furthermore, cloud service providers often offer compliance certifications for their platforms and services, such as the AWS Compliance Program and the Microsoft Azure Compliance Program, which certify that the provider's infrastructure meets specific regulatory requirements and industry standards, and CLI commands such as cloud governance tools can help organizations assess their compliance with cloud provider certifications by monitoring their cloud resources and configurations. In summary, compliance frameworks for edge computing *implementations play a vital role in helping organizations navigate the complex landscape of regulatory requirements and industry standards, and by leveraging CLI commands and techniques tailored to specific frameworks, organizations can achieve and maintain compliance effectively while minimizing legal and regulatory risks.*

Chapter 9: Future Trends in Industry 4.0 and Edge Computing

Emerging technologies are revolutionizing Industry 4.0, paving the way for unprecedented levels of automation, efficiency, and connectivity in manufacturing and beyond, with advancements such as artificial intelligence (AI) and machine learning (ML) playing a central role in transforming traditional industrial processes into intelligent, data-driven operations. CLI commands can be used to deploy AI and ML algorithms on edge devices, enabling real-time data analysis and decision-making at the edge of the network, thereby reducing latency and enhancing overall system performance. Additionally, the Internet of Things (IoT) is another key enabler of Industry 4.0, allowing for the interconnection of physical devices and sensors to collect and exchange data, with CLI commands facilitating the deployment and management of IoT devices and gateways in industrial environments. Furthermore, 5G technology promises to unlock new opportunities for Industry 4.0 by providing ultra-fast, low-

latency connectivity that supports a wide range of applications, from remote monitoring and predictive maintenance to collaborative robotics and augmented reality, with CLI commands enabling network configuration and optimization for 5G deployments. Moreover, edge computing is emerging as a critical infrastructure component for Industry 4.0, allowing for the processing and analysis of data closer to the source, thereby reducing bandwidth requirements and enabling real-time decision-making in distributed industrial environments, with CLI commands facilitating the deployment and management of edge computing resources and applications. Additionally, blockchain technology is gaining traction in Industry 4.0, offering secure and transparent data management solutions for supply chain tracking, product authentication, and digital payments, with CLI commands enabling the deployment and configuration of blockchain networks and smart contracts in industrial settings. Furthermore, augmented reality (AR) and virtual reality (VR) technologies are transforming the way workers interact with machines and processes in Industry 4.0, providing immersive training experiences, remote assistance capabilities, and visualization tools for complex tasks, with CLI commands enabling the deployment and management of AR/VR applications and devices in industrial environments. Moreover, additive manufacturing, or 3D printing, is revolutionizing the production process in Industry 4.0, allowing for the rapid prototyping and customization of parts and products, with CLI commands facilitating the setup and operation of 3D printers and associated software. Additionally, digital twins are becoming increasingly important in Industry 4.0, providing virtual representations of physical assets and processes that enable predictive maintenance, optimization, and simulation, with CLI commands enabling the deployment and synchronization of digital twin models with real-world data sources. Furthermore, cognitive computing technologies, such as natural language processing (NLP) and computer vision, are enhancing human-machine interaction and decision-making in Industry 4.0, enabling intelligent automation and personalized user experiences, with CLI commands facilitating the deployment and integration of cognitive computing systems into industrial workflows. In

summary, emerging technologies are driving the transformation of Industry 4.0, offering new capabilities and opportunities for innovation across a wide range of industries, and by leveraging CLI commands to deploy and manage these technologies, organizations can accelerate their digital transformation efforts and stay ahead of the curve in the fast-paced world of modern manufacturing.
Anticipating future trends in edge computing involves closely monitoring technological advancements and industry developments to forecast how edge computing will continue to evolve and shape various sectors. One significant trend is the proliferation of edge devices, which are expected to become more numerous and diverse, spanning from smartphones and IoT sensors to autonomous vehicles and industrial machinery. Deploying edge devices in diverse environments requires careful consideration of factors such as power consumption, processing capabilities, and connectivity, with CLI commands being instrumental in provisioning and managing these devices. Additionally, edge computing architectures are anticipated to become more distributed and decentralized, with edge nodes being deployed closer to the point of

data generation to minimize latency and bandwidth usage, necessitating the use of CLI commands to configure and orchestrate these distributed systems effectively. Furthermore, edge computing is expected to play a crucial role in enabling real-time analytics and decision-making across a wide range of applications, including smart cities, autonomous vehicles, healthcare, and manufacturing, with CLI commands facilitating the deployment and management of edge analytics platforms and frameworks. Moreover, edge computing is poised to integrate more seamlessly with cloud computing infrastructures, forming hybrid architectures that leverage the strengths of both edge and cloud technologies to optimize performance, scalability, and cost-effectiveness, with CLI commands being used to configure and maintain these hybrid environments. Additionally, edge computing is anticipated to drive advancements in artificial intelligence (AI) and machine learning (ML) algorithms, enabling edge devices to perform increasingly sophisticated data processing tasks autonomously, with CLI commands being employed to deploy and update AI/ML models on edge devices efficiently. Furthermore, edge computing is expected to continue expanding its footprint in critical infrastructure sectors such as energy, transportation, and healthcare, where reliability, security, and resilience are paramount, necessitating the use of CLI commands to ensure the robustness and integrity of edge deployments. Moreover, edge computing is likely to spur innovation in edge-native applications and services, with developers leveraging edge resources to deliver novel experiences and functionalities to end-users, with CLI commands playing a vital role in the development, testing, and deployment of edge applications. Additionally, edge computing is anticipated to drive new business models and revenue streams, with organizations monetizing their edge infrastructure and data assets through value-added services, subscription models, and pay-per-use offerings, with CLI commands facilitating the provisioning and billing of these services. Furthermore, edge computing is expected to foster greater collaboration and interoperability among ecosystem partners, enabling seamless integration of edge technologies into existing workflows and systems, with CLI commands being used to configure and manage the interfaces and protocols required for interoperability. Moreover, edge computing is poised to address emerging challenges such as privacy, security, and data governance, with organizations adopting encryption, access controls, and data anonymization techniques to protect sensitive information at the edge, with CLI commands being employed to enforce security policies and monitor compliance. Additionally, edge computing is anticipated to drive advancements in edge-native development tools and frameworks, empowering developers to build and deploy edge applications more efficiently and effectively, with CLI commands providing the interface for developers to interact with these tools and frameworks. Furthermore, edge computing is likely to catalyze innovation in edge infrastructure technologies such as edge gateways, edge routers, and edge servers, with vendors investing in research and development to improve the performance, reliability, and scalability of edge hardware components, with CLI commands being used to configure and optimize these infrastructure elements. In summary, anticipating future trends in edge computing requires a holistic understanding of technological, market, and regulatory factors, *with CLI commands serving as a critical tool for implementing and managing edge computing solutions in diverse environments and use cases.*

Chapter 10: Case Studies and Success Stories

Examining successful implementations of Industry 4.0 and edge computing provides valuable insights into the transformative potential of these technologies across various sectors. In manufacturing, for example, companies are leveraging edge computing to optimize production processes, improve product quality, and reduce downtime, with CLI commands being used to deploy edge computing solutions on factory floors. By integrating sensors, actuators, and other IoT devices into their production lines, manufacturers can collect real-time data on equipment performance, environmental conditions, and product quality, allowing them to identify inefficiencies and make data-driven decisions to improve operations. Additionally, edge computing enables manufacturers to implement predictive maintenance strategies, where CLI commands are utilized to deploy machine learning models that analyze sensor data to predict equipment failures before they occur, thereby minimizing downtime and reducing maintenance costs.

Moreover, edge computing facilitates the implementation of autonomous robotics and automation systems in manufacturing, with CLI commands being used to orchestrate robotic workflows and coordinate tasks across distributed edge nodes. In the transportation sector, edge computing is revolutionizing logistics and supply chain management by enabling real-time tracking and monitoring of vehicles, shipments, and assets, with CLI commands facilitating the deployment of edge computing solutions on trucks, trains, ships, and warehouses. By equipping vehicles and containers with edge devices, transportation companies can collect and analyze data on fuel consumption, vehicle performance, and cargo conditions in real-time, allowing them to optimize routes, reduce fuel costs, and improve delivery times. Additionally, edge computing enables transportation companies to implement dynamic routing and scheduling algorithms that adjust delivery routes and pickup times based on traffic conditions, weather forecasts, and other real-time factors, with CLI commands being used to update routing policies and algorithms on-the-fly. Furthermore, edge computing is transforming healthcare delivery by enabling remote patient monitoring, telemedicine consultations, and personalized treatment plans, with CLI commands being utilized to deploy edge computing solutions in hospitals, clinics, and remote care facilities. By equipping patients with wearable sensors and mobile health devices, healthcare providers can collect and analyze patient data in real-time, allowing them to monitor vital signs, detect early warning signs of health problems, and intervene proactively to prevent complications. Additionally, edge computing enables healthcare providers to deliver personalized treatment plans and interventions based on individual patient data and medical histories, with CLI commands being used to deploy AI-based decision support systems and clinical decision-making tools. Moreover, edge computing is enhancing energy efficiency and sustainability in smart buildings and cities by enabling real-time monitoring and optimization of energy consumption, with CLI commands facilitating the deployment of edge computing solutions in building management systems and smart grid infrastructure. By collecting and analyzing data from sensors, meters, and IoT devices installed in buildings, utilities, and infrastructure, cities can identify opportunities to reduce energy waste, improve resource utilization, and lower carbon emissions, with CLI commands being used to implement energy-saving measures and control systems. Additionally, edge computing enables cities to implement intelligent transportation systems, smart street lighting, and environmental monitoring networks that optimize traffic flow, reduce congestion, and improve air quality, with CLI commands being used to deploy and manage these interconnected edge networks. Furthermore, edge computing is revolutionizing retail and e-commerce by enabling personalized shopping experiences, real-time inventory management, and supply chain optimization, with CLI commands being utilized to deploy edge computing solutions in retail stores, warehouses, and distribution centers. By integrating sensors, cameras, and AI-powered analytics into their stores and supply chains, retailers can collect and analyze data on customer behavior, product preferences, and inventory levels in real-time, allowing them to offer personalized recommendations, optimize shelf layouts, and reduce stockouts. Additionally, edge computing enables retailers to implement automated checkout systems, inventory tracking solutions, *and last-mile delivery services that streamline operations and enhance customer satisfaction, with CLI commands being used to configure and manage these edge-based retail solutions. In summary, examining successful implementations of Industry 4.0 and edge computing across various sectors highlights the transformative potential of these technologies in optimizing operations, improving efficiency, and delivering value to businesses and society as a whole, with CLI commands playing a crucial role in deploying, managing, and optimizing edge computing solutions.*

Analyzing case studies and success stories yields valuable insights and lessons learned that can inform future deployments and implementations of edge computing solutions, with CLI commands often being instrumental in replicating successful strategies and configurations. One key lesson is the importance of understanding the unique requirements and constraints of each use case or application when designing and deploying edge computing solutions. By conducting thorough assessments of the specific challenges, objectives, and stakeholders involved, organizations can tailor their edge architectures and strategies to address the most pressing needs and deliver the greatest value, with CLI commands being used to customize configurations and parameters based on these requirements. Moreover, case studies highlight the critical role of collaboration and partnership in driving successful edge computing initiatives, as organizations often need to work with technology vendors, system integrators, and domain experts to overcome technical hurdles, navigate regulatory requirements, and achieve business goals, with CLI commands facilitating the integration and interoperability of diverse technologies and platforms. Additionally, case studies underscore the importance of continuous monitoring, optimization, and iteration in maintaining the performance, reliability, and security of edge computing environments over time, with CLI commands enabling administrators and operators to deploy updates, patches, and security fixes, as well as to fine-tune configurations and parameters to adapt to changing conditions and requirements. Furthermore, case studies demonstrate the value of leveraging scalable and flexible architectures that can accommodate evolving workloads, data volumes, and user demands, with CLI commands being used to scale resources up or down, provision new edge nodes or services, and orchestrate distributed workflows dynamically in response to changing conditions or priorities. Another important lesson is the need to prioritize security and compliance in edge computing deployments, as edge environments often involve distributed infrastructure, diverse devices, and heterogeneous networks that can introduce new vulnerabilities and risks, with CLI commands being used to implement encryption, authentication, access controls, and other security measures to protect sensitive data and assets from unauthorized access, manipulation, or exfiltration. Moreover, case studies highlight the importance of robust data management and governance practices in ensuring the integrity, availability, and accuracy of data collected, processed, and stored at the edge, with CLI commands enabling administrators and operators to enforce data policies, manage data lifecycles, and ensure compliance with regulatory requirements and industry standards. Additionally, case studies emphasize the value of automation and orchestration in streamlining operations, reducing human error, and maximizing efficiency in edge computing environments, with CLI commands being used to automate routine tasks, configure workflows, and enforce policies programmatically across distributed infrastructure and devices. Furthermore, case studies underscore the importance of user experience and satisfaction in driving adoption and acceptance of edge computing solutions, as end-users and stakeholders expect seamless, reliable, and responsive experiences that meet their needs and expectations, with CLI commands being used to optimize performance, latency, and reliability metrics to deliver superior user experiences and outcomes. Another key lesson is the value of data analytics and insights in extracting value and generating actionable intelligence from edge-generated data, with CLI commands being used to deploy analytics tools, algorithms, and models that can analyze, visualize, and interpret data in real-time to support decision-making, optimization, and innovation. Moreover, case studies highlight the importance of resilience and fault tolerance in ensuring the continuity and availability of critical services and applications in edge computing environments, with CLI commands being used to implement redundancy, failover, and disaster recovery *mechanisms that can mitigate the impact of hardware failures, network outages, and other disruptions. Additionally, case studies underscore the need for regulatory compliance and risk management in edge computing deployments, as organizations must adhere to relevant laws, regulations, and standards governing data privacy, security, and governance, with CLI commands being used to enforce policies, monitor compliance, and audit activities to demonstrate adherence to regulatory requirements and industry best practices. In summary, lessons learned from case studies and success stories in edge computing provide valuable guidance and insights for organizations embarking on their own edge initiatives, with CLI commands playing a crucial role in deploying, managing, and securing edge environments to achieve desired outcomes and deliver tangible value to stakeholders and end-users.*

Conclusion

In this comprehensive book bundle, "Edge Computing 101: Novice to Pro," readers have embarked on a journey from the foundational principles of edge computing to advanced techniques and practical applications across various industries.

Book 1, "Edge Computing Fundamentals: A Beginner's Guide to Distributed Systems," laid the groundwork by introducing readers to the core concepts of distributed computing, providing them with a solid understanding of the underlying principles and architectures that form the basis of edge computing.

Building upon this foundation, Book 2, "Edge Computing Architectures: Design Principles and Best Practices," delved deeper into the design considerations and architectural patterns essential for building robust and scalable edge computing systems. Readers gained insights into key components, deployment models, and optimization strategies required to design effective edge architectures.

Book 3, "Advanced Edge Computing: Scalability, Security, and Optimization Strategies," equipped readers with advanced techniques and strategies to overcome scalability challenges, enhance security measures, and optimize performance in edge environments. Through real-world examples and case studies, readers learned how to address complex issues and achieve optimal outcomes in their edge computing deployments.

Finally, Book 4, "Edge Computing in Industry 4.0: Practical Applications and Future Trends," explored the practical applications of edge computing across various industries, with a focus on Industry 4.0. Readers gained insights into how edge computing is revolutionizing manufacturing, supply chain management, smart cities, healthcare, and more, while also examining future trends and emerging technologies shaping the landscape of edge computing.

As readers conclude their journey through this book bundle, they emerge with a comprehensive *understanding of edge computing, from its fundamental concepts to advanced techniques and practical applications. Armed with this knowledge, they are equipped to navigate the complexities of edge computing and harness its transformative potential to drive innovation, efficiency, and competitiveness in the digital age.*